SOUL CARE • SC

WALK ON WATER

COMPANION JOURNAL

DR. ELIZABETH FULGARO

HOLY SPIRIT PRESS | RESCUE, CA

Walk on Water Companion Journal

Permissions
Holy Spirit Press an imprint of
Eagles Nest Foundation, Inc. 501(c)3
PO Box 130
Rescue, CA 95672

ISBN: 978-1-961762-08-4

Manufactured in the U.S.A. 2025

Edited by Lois E. Olena

Cover Design: Amy Cole

Artwork: Margaret Hart

DEDICATION

To you, as you spend time daily
with song prayers and this companion journal,
and God meets you there.

CONTENTS

APPENDIX

WELCOME

Welcome to the *Walk on Water Companion Journal.* Released in autumn 2007, *Walk on Water* was my second album. Shortly, after beginning the first, *Ascend in Worship*, I recognized a deep need for song prayer for when life does not look like what you thought it would. No matter your circumstances, you need to be able to approach God authentically as the psalmists did. *Walk on Water* does worship God in the reality of His sovereignty and awareness of His spiritual throne room. However, there is also room for your hurt, sorrow and questions. When you pay God homage like this, you will experience Him in an expanding manner. With repetition you will sense Him near working on your heart. Not with superficial platitudes like so many people, but with sometimes hard realities couched in true consolation.

Of course, you do not have to listen to *Walk on Water* daily to benefit from the Companion Journal, just as you do not need the journal to benefit from the spiritual practice of daily listening to song prayers on the album. However, I fervently hope you find the information and stories contained in these album-specific Companion Journals useful on your journey closer to God.

The purpose of this album-specific journaling experience is to accompany your daily listening. If this is your first Companion Journal, I recommend you read all of Part One which precedes the daily reflections and journaling pages to get familiar with the spiritual practice of daily listening to song prayers. If you have used an album-specific Companion Journal before, then feel free to jump ahead to Part Two and right into the reflections and journaling pages.

MY STORY

In 2004, friends spontaneously prayed over me that I would begin composing song prayers God wanted released on the earth. In 2005, I experienced an unmistakable message from God through a vision to develop some of the song prayers for delivery to military service members.

Song prayers are songs that are prayers. In the years since, I have developed over 250 on 25+ albums and distributed over 10,000 albums to military service members, military families, families of fallen service members, veterans, and people amid other life battles. Each album features song prayers centered around a nuanced theme to give listeners the ability to approach God through listening to song prayers in varied life circumstances and states of mind.

As I went through the production process for each album, I noticed that by engaging with the song prayers regularly and repeatedly, using them as prayer for connection with God, I felt strengthened and transformed both spiritually and emotionally. The song prayers aimed my thoughts at God and caused me to be present to Him. I experienced God's interaction in response. I was not alone in this experience. As I made the albums available, I received feedback through verbal comments, written notes, and social media interaction from listeners. They reported a similar building of capacity for resilience through repeatedly offering these song prayers to God while listening with intentionality, reflection, and an openness to His interaction. Not all those who received them as a gift listened to the song prayers. For some, it was simply receiving a gift that mattered because they felt more seen and valued. However, where recipients put the song prayers to use, they reported being changed in positive ways like what I had experienced. What was happening?

DOING THE RESEARCH

Using songs that are prayers toward connection with God is not novel. In fact, during recent decades in certain branches of Christianity some have emphasized specifically integrating congregational music periods of offering song prayers to God communally during regular services, with an expectation of interaction from God in response. What made my experiences and the experiences of those near me unique was that the song prayers were listened to *repeatedly and offered reflectively* during private, one-on-one time with God. Utilizing the song prayers in this way seemed to open a liminal space—a threshold—between the physical and spiritual realms, with interaction from God in response. We could neither control nor predict the nature of God's interaction, but the transformational outcomes were real, practical and personal.

Additionally, what was experienced through the power of listening to the song prayers seemed less affected by use of one song played one time. Instead, listening to the song prayers repetitively for consistent blocks of time (like listening to an album, LP, or playlist) seemed to result in the most beneficial outcomes. The observations of positive outcomes from song prayer listening had been no more than anecdotal but remained intriguing—especially when combined with the ongoing challenge communicated to me by several military contacts asking what I would do for those engaged in battles for their mental, emotional and spiritual health, not just physical. In my work on my Master of Practical Theology (MPT) degree, where my study focused on emotional healing, I began to consider whether listening to song prayers could serve as a type of CAM (complementary and alternative medicine), where the spiritual practice of regular, repetitive listening was another form of soul care. What if I had stumbled onto a type of spiritual practice involving song prayer listening versus reading, writing, meditation, etc.? What if the outcomes experienced by the few individuals that I knew engaging in the practice were not extraordinary but to be expected?

I decided to do research and find out. During 2022–2023, I embarked on a doctoral study to increase understanding regarding how song prayers influenced emotional well-being. Four women veterans committed to listening for a block of at least twenty minutes per day for a minimum of twenty-eight consecutive days to a customized playlist of my song prayers and to keep track of their sense of emotional well-being before and after listening. The results of the qualitative study showed that regular, reflective listening to song prayers increases resilience, which augments emotional well-being. Each participant received specific insights, experienced inner changes, or sensed specific interaction from God, which helped her thrive more.

The study participants also unanimously encouraged me to make the spiritual practice of listening to song prayers known and easily available for you, too. Thus, I have published a book on the study, *Soul*

Care·Song Prayers: A Spiritual Practice toward Resilience and Well-Being and album-specific Companion Journals to accompany daily listening like this one. The purpose of these journals is to foster the self-reflection for you which participants found so useful in the study. You will find this album on most streaming services as well as under playlists on my YouTube channel (https://www.YouTube.com/@elizabethfulgaro). CDs are also available for purchase. Additionally, with the Eagles Nest Soul Care Song Prayers app available in both smartphone stores for free download, you can listen to *Walk on Water* anytime uninterrupted by commercials, which is vital for daily listening to have its full potential proactive effect.

What made my experiences and the experiences of those near me unique was that the song prayers were listened to *repeatedly and offered reflectively* during private, one-on-one time with God.

LET'S GO!

Part One of the journal introduces you to the spiritual practice to make it easier to implement it for yourself. Part Two provides a thirty-day journal with reflections for each day related to the *Walk on Water* album, including how some of the song prayers came to be, what was happening at the time, and what God was teaching me. The journal concludes with an appendix listing additional resources and providing extra journaling pages. All of this together is to help you process what you have experienced through these special listening times as well as in life as a result.

I am so excited you are here! Let's get started on this next part of your inner healing journey toward greater wholeness and activation through increased focus on the presence of God and openness to His interaction in your life. As I write to you, it is both the beginning of Passover and

Palm Sunday. How significant for your *Walk on Water* listening where the focus is what God is doing and what He promises while leaning into Him during times which are difficult to understand and hurt your heart.

May you have blessed listening and blessed God encounters!

— Dr. Elizabeth Fulgaro
El Dorado County, California
Passover and Palm Sunday,
April 13, 2025

PART ONE

THE SPIRITUAL PRACTICE OF DAILY LISTENING TO SONG PRAYERS

You are invited to a liminal space—a literal threshold between the spiritual and physical realms—where God wants to interact with you. My research shows that one method to create such a space in your everyday life is through the daily spiritual practice of listening to song prayers. The term *song prayers* refers to songs that are prayers, or melodies with lyrics, which seek to converse with God.

You were made for connection with God. You are a spiritual as well as a physical, emotional, and social being. The connection God seeks with you, and which will feed and nurture you from the inside out, goes beyond congregational gatherings. God also longs to meet with you one on one. We all have a vital spiritual need for this connection. Simultaneously, it is often a missing component of daily living.

As you know, life can be tough. Time to connect with God and receive what He has for you can prove hard to find. Many common spiritual practices such as reading your Bible or participating in a Bible study primarily engage your reason. There is nothing wrong with this! However, for human beings, acquisition of knowledge goes beyond memorization of informational facts. We receive true knowledge through both reason and emotions. Music listening connects with both and facilitates receipt of knowledge at a deeper level than engaging with words alone. Music is its own language and has been used going back beyond what history can fully document as a preferred means with which to seek to connect with God.

What God has for you comes most through relationship, and as in any other relationship, you open yourself to all He offers when you choose to spend time with Him. When you do, you feel better and function better.

Song prayers have been used throughout the ages as a means of honoring God where connection and interaction result. The forms of song prayers have varied through the centuries and include genres such as psalms, hymns, and contemporary praise and worship songs. Each of these has served as a means of regularly and repetitively honoring God where connection with Him and interaction from Him has provided an expected and experienced outcome. The response from God, which cannot be regulated, predicted, or commanded by human beings, seems to consistently occur both in ways you can expect as well as in ways that demolish the boundaries of what you thought possible.

Through repetition of song prayers, people and their outlook on whatever they were going through were changed as they gained greater understanding of God, His perspective, and His promises. Additionally, they also experienced interaction from God occurring in ways they could not fully explain. These ways addressed their needs, though, often in ways beyond what they could have imagined.

They had a sense of enhanced well-being. In the liminal space through regular use of song prayers, people had encounters with God by which they felt strengthened and healed and came into a place of greater thriving. (You can learn more specifics about this in my doctoral study[1] and book, *Soul Care·Song Prayers: A Spiritual Practice Toward Resilience and Well-Being.*[2])

It is common not to have a lot of room for God in our mind moment-by moment. Our brain space gets consumed by other thoughts. You really cannot think a lot more than one thought at a time. (I'll let a neuroscientist address that.) Yet, truly you cannot hear the quiet infusion of God's voice into your own thoughts when your thoughts are already whirling in hectic or anxiety. To meet with God and receive

1 My doctoral study, "The Influence of Listening to Song Prayers on the Resilience of Women Veterans," is available on Google Scholar. The study is also featured in my book, *Soul Care·Song Prayers: A Spiritual Practice Toward Resilience and Well-Being.*

2 Scan the QR code for a link to *Soul Care·Song Prayers: A Spiritual Practice Toward Resilience and Well-Being* on Amazon.

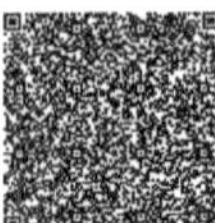

from Him, you need to spend focused time with Him. God will not chase you down and insist that you need Him as you run the other way because you are just so busy or distracted. You must choose to stop.

You must choose to stop.

The daily practice of listening to song prayers helps. The ultimate purpose of the song prayers is to give God the honor and glory (praise or credit) He is due. Through your pause to offer song prayers, you acknowledge, "Wow, You really are God and in charge of all things. How amazing is this? How amazing are You!" As you do, you welcome God to come closer and be more intimate with you. You are seeking God, and He promises that if you seek Him, He will be found by you. He promises to *inhabit* your song prayers— to come that near!

By reflecting on the lyrics in the song prayers as you listen, your mind becomes filled with thoughts aimed toward God, and the liminal space is created where your being encounters His in the way that He determines is best. You have made room for Him, and He delights to respond to you. He has longed for greater interaction with you— to care for you more specifically. He wants to fill you up with His Spirit, described in the Bible as the Living Water and Water of Life, so that out of that well, He can flow through you to touch others. You do not fill this empty well within you. He does. Focused time with God—where listening to song prayers enhances that interaction—creates an atmosphere that beckons encounter and positions your heart to receive from Him.

My doctoral research showed, when you listen to an album or a playlist like *Walk on Water* for at least twenty uninterrupted minutes daily for at least twenty-eight consecutive days as a spiritual practice, your emotional well-being, spiritual well-being and resilience in everyday life are strengthened. There are spiritual, practical, psychological and neuroscientific reasons for this, which relate to how research also increasingly understands music as medicine.

The term *song prayers* is my own, developed because I sensed a lack of an overarching, descriptively sufficient term for what I was discovering. (I hope it will become your term, too.) Originally, I called the songs I was writing "worship songs"—songs whereby you worship God because the lyrics of each adored Him. However, I also recognized the need for a term understandable to more people. Most of my songs fit under the contemporary worship music genre. However, I was cognizant that not everyone understood the word *worship* in conjunction with merely particular types of songs. Many viewed worship as the thrust of their entire church service. The term "worship" as referring just to a particular type of music could be nebulous and potentially confusing. Additionally, as I did the historical portion of the research, I found that through the centuries, the mystical, transformative effect from interaction with God as a result of reaching toward Him through worshipful music transcended the more recent contemporary praise and worship genre. For instance, it was documented how people through the ages had worshiped God musically utilizing psalms, hymns, and other genres and had similar effects. I developed the term "song prayers" to be an overarching and inclusive term under which all genres of music could fall which seek to honor, adore, and pay homage to God, whether with vocals or purely instrumental. Song prayers: songs that are prayers.

Know that as you choose to engage in the spiritual practice of daily listening, generally it is not the first or even second time that you set aside the time to listen that you will experience God. Further, to the extent that you make the practice your habit, make no mistake— God will interact with you. That is His promise. With time, your awareness of Him becomes more pronounced.

Humans tend to gravitate toward music we already know. Yet, frequently you may be unfamiliar with the song prayers featured on an album as you begin your twenty-eight-day daily listening focus. Persist! With daily listening each new collection of song prayers will soon become your own!

Additionally, you may find you need different song prayers for different days. Begin with *Walk on Water* and stick with it a while to see if these song prayers become part of you. But if you find they are not quite right for where you find yourself emotionally right now, please try a different album or playlist! You can still continue with the journaling pages, even though the reflections are specifically drawn from the stories and revelations related to development of *Walk on Water.*

The spiritual practice of listening to song prayers daily is just that: a spiritual practice. Some days you will want to do this discipline, and some days you won't. If you persist, though, you will be rewarded! Research shows the benefits through interaction with God that come because of listening to song prayers are not immediate, but don't quit. Keep going and be surprised at what God will do. Restart if you find you have stopped. This *Walk on Water Companion Journal* serves as a tool to make engaging in the spiritual practice of listening to song prayers easier so you can reap the most productive benefits.

Listening to song prayers as a daily spiritual practice does not replace other means of nurturing your relationship with God but augments these—and it's so easy! Let's look at how to implement and make the most of your daily listening.

QUICK OVERVIEW OF WHAT TO DO

The spiritual practice of listening to song prayers consists of five simple steps: Select, Reflect, Listen, Reflect, Repeat.

1. *Select your song prayers.* Don't think too hard. Let it be fun. Let your feelings and intuition, which often are God speaking to you, lead. This Companion Journal is geared toward *Walk on Water.* You can adjust your list day by day as you learn and experience (and feel the need) for more or for something different. Be random. Be spontaneous. Don't worry. You cannot get this wrong so long as you start to spend song prayer listening time each day.

2. *Reflect for a moment before listening.* How do you feel before you begin when you subjectively measure your well-being on a scale of 1 to 10 where one is worst and 10 is best?

3. *Listen now!* Give it at least twenty consecutive minutes.

4. *Reflect for a moment.* How do you feel now? Rate your emotional well-being again. (If you do not feel like reflecting, that is OK, too.) God will still be at work in you in ways you do notice as time goes on!

5. *Repeat. If you miss a day, there is no need to stress.* Just start again tomorrow. If you find you miss too many days, stop, and ask what's not working. Reflect. Maybe adjust where you implement the song prayer listening in your day and start again.

Remembering these steps is the most essential information. Keep reading for additional detail and tips regarding the spiritual practice of listening to song prayers or head to Part Two to begin your first day of listening and your journaling pages.

DETAILS OF LISTENING TO SONG PRAYERS AS PART OF YOUR SOUL CARE

CREATE THE SPACE; CREATE THE HABIT

The women veterans who participated in my doctoral research were asked to listen to song prayers in a block of at least twenty minutes per day for at least twenty-eight consecutive days. To be honest, the number of minutes per day and the number of consecutive days were not a rigid formula. However, certain principles did undergird the recommendation that this is how you start. To receive what God wants to impart as you engage in the spiritual practice of listening to song prayers daily, listening needs to become a habit.

In the research, each participant stated separately that the greatest effect from song prayer listening did not happen the first day. Only after participants listened daily for a while did they either begin to notice changes; things happened that told them transformation was taking place on a unique and personal level, which was benefitting them greatly. Thus, you will want to use the song prayers regularly and commit sufficient time daily over a duration of days or weeks for interaction with God to become more palpable. I hope you become so addicted to listening daily to song prayers that you will adopt the spiritual practice for the rest of your life as part of your soul care! However, even if initially you commit to try it for just twenty-eight days, you are reaching into a duration shown to contribute to habit development. Once daily listening develops into a normative habit, it can feel almost effortless, and you will no longer have to remember to squeeze it in somewhere. This spiritual practice finds its place as you mentally prioritize it.

You will find yourself listening for longer each day as time goes on because you have begun to experience the extraordinary presence of God.

The daily length of listening should be long enough to quiet the mind and re-orient your thoughts to God. Frequently this effect is not instantaneous the moment you begin listening. As you begin your daily time of song prayer, your mind may already feel naturally abuzz with other thoughts. Instead of trying to empty your mind, as you listen to the song prayers they will help clear out 'thought cobwebs,' which can cloud and even block clear reception of what God wants to impart. Listening to song prayers hones your thoughts in on God as other distractions are pushed out of your mind far away; then, you can be present to God in the way He is present to you. Now you have created that liminal space where you attend to Him, and He interacts with you—both in ways you might immediately recognize and in those that remain hidden until later.

My own transformational experiences utilizing the song prayers to connect with God usually occurred through listening to at least an album of songs at a time. Albums tend to average thirty-five to forty minutes in length, so what I really want to do is ask you to commit to listen that long daily. When you are not familiar with how good this spiritual practice can be, the idea of committing to listen for that length of time may seem daunting, discouraging and just too long as you begin. On the other hand, I also know that five or ten minutes of listening will not prove long enough for God to wash over you so that you receive from Him what He wants to give you. God is not a drive-through or a microwave! You need time to focus on the song prayers to help quiet your mind and push out lesser thoughts, thereby orienting your mind and heart to God. Thus, my request that you listen for at least twenty minutes per day is a compromise of sorts, which seems to work. At first, the practice of listening to song prayers regularly may feel artificial, mechanical, or prescriptive. Just keep going. Eventually, if you are like the study participants, you will find yourself listening for longer each day as time goes on because you have begun to experience the extraordinary presence of God through connecting with Him through listening to the song prayers.

SELECT, REFLECT, LISTEN, REFLECT, REPEAT

SELECT

For two decades, God has had me creating song prayers, now available for you to use in their original form on albums (CDs and LPs), by way of playlists I have created (or through ones you will create yourself), and on various streaming services. The Eagles Nest Soul Care Song Prayers app enables you to listen daily and keep track of how you are doing.

The song prayers the Holy Spirit had me create are unique. Each album is based on a slightly different theme the Lord whispered to my heart before I began actively listening for wisps of the songs He wanted created. Each step of every song prayer's development has been bathed in prayer, asking the Holy Spirit to use the song prayers specifically in the lives of listeners in the way He knows each listener needs. I have also sought God's direction regarding melody, arrangement, lyrics, and harmonies. All the lyrics talk directly *to* God, paying Him respect, homage, and adoration—versus lyrics which tell about Him.

Walk on Water was the second album. It includes song prayers with themes which worship God in the beauty of His holiness, as well as those with which to approach God authentically when what has happened confounds you, your heart hurts, His answer seems to tarry, or you are in deep sorrow.

REFLECT

The main thrust of this book is found in Part Two. Between the daily album-focused reflections and guided journaling pages, you are encouraged to self-reflect as part of your spiritual practice of daily listening to song prayers. You do not have to use these pages. You can also make mental notes, use audio notes on your smart phone, or write out notes in your own journal of a different sort. You also do not have to self-reflect to receive from God through the spiritual practice of listening daily to song prayer. However, research has shown that a little self-reflection enhances the benefits of the spiritual practice.

The usefulness of self-reflection has long been known. In the early Christian Church, believers integrated a practice of self-reflection side by side with reading or listening to the Bible, which made the one engaging with the material more available for interaction from God. This ancient practice, called *lectio divina* (which means divine reading), was found so useful that it continues today. The spiritual practice of *lectio divina* commonly is described featuring four steps, "lectio" (read a short passage of Scripture, "meditatio", (reflect) "contemplatio" (contemplate) and "oratio" (pray).

When you combine self-reflection and spiritual listening with the spiritual practice of listening to song prayers, it develops into something you could describe as *audio divina.* You can use the journaling pages to begin to record the thoughts that come to you and what you experience while listening.

At a minimum, my doctoral study participants found useful the research study requirement that they keep track of their subjective sense of emotional well-being both before and after their listening periods each day. So, this is where you can start, too, either by using the journaling pages that follow, the smartphone app, or your own system. The following pages make it simple. Open to the next day's journaling pages. Log the date. Right before you listen, check in with yourself. On a scale of 1 to 10, where 1 is lowest and 10 is highest, how are you feeling right now? Write down your starting number for the day in the indicated location on your journal page for the day. Now comes the great part! It's time to listen to song prayers.

LISTEN

I recommend that you commit to listening daily for a block of at least twenty minutes per day for at least twenty-eight consecutive days. Longer is even better. The average song length is three to four minutes, so listening to about seven or eight songs should take you close to completing twenty minutes of prayerful listening per day. Each album features between ten and twelve song prayers. Playlists of course can be customized. Some days some songs will hit home more than others. You might find yourself listening to one or two songs over and over because that's what allows God to minister to you best.

Keep this in mind. You do not have to listen to the song prayers on your album/playlist in a particular order. You can listen solely to those songs that speak to you now and set aside the others. You can listen to a particular song repeatedly. You do not have to listen to songs that do not appeal to you at all. The song prayers can be listened to in whatever order seems best for the day. Do with the song prayers whatever fits you best in the moment. The Holy Spirit, who is the presence of

God here with you now, can direct you in choosing. He can teach you to hear His inner prompts so you can follow where He is leading.

By participating in these song prayers through listening, you are—in effect—offering these to God as you listen. Since God seeks connection with you, listening to the song prayers and offering them to Him as a form of adoration puts you in a position of seeking God in return. When you do, He promises to be found by you. He wants relationship with you that is personal and growing. He created conversation as a key means of connection between human beings and God. We call this form of communication with God prayer. Song prayers initiate your openness to this conversation with God and interaction with Him in a manner that has biblical and historical precedent.

Since an object of your listening to these song prayers is to place yourself in a liminal space to experience interaction from God, it is vital that the means by which you listen remain free of interference from advertisements. The best way to listen is by CD, LP, or the free Eagles Nest Soul Care Song Prayers app. However, if you do utilize a streaming service, make sure you listen without commercial interruptions. Advertisements break the flow of connection with God and pull your focus away from thoughts of Him to something lower, thereby disrupting with the place the song prayers are helping to create within you where you can listen for and hear from God. Obviously, you can restore connection with God, but it is unlikely to reach the intensity possible when your attention remains stayed on Him.

Song prayer listening with intention and reflection does not mean you have to stop everything and just sit somewhere and listen. What you do or do not do when you listen depends on what helps you focus best on the song prayers. For instance, sometimes for me it is listening as I drive. For others, cooking or going for a walk may help them focus. For still others, they welcome the time to stop, lie down, and rest as they listen.

You'll also notice doodling space on the journaling pages with a small doodling prompt in the lower corner to get you going. Most important is to do what helps you listen to the song prayers best and be more open to God as you do. You can also journal thoughts which come to mind in this space. (There are also a few extra blank journaling pages in the Appendix as well.).

Let the song prayers wash over you and soak into you mind, body, and soul.

Common to all the varied methods is letting the song prayers wash over you and soak into you mind, body, and soul. To do this, your mind needs to remain free of other distractions and focuses, so you cannot be doing activities that require your brain to focus on thoughts outside what is going on in the songs. You can be active, but your brain must remain in a passive, open state and ready to receive. The Bible talks about the presence of God through the Spirit of God like a stream or river of living water that comes into the deserts of existence and brings life. There is growth, thriving, and even harvest instead of parched barrenness. Listening to song prayers invites the river of God's refreshing into your own desert.

Now, if you miss a day of song prayer listening, please do not stress or beat yourself up. Just start again tomorrow. If you are trying to complete a twenty-eight-day focus, just add that day to the end of what would have been your twenty-eighth day. If you really get off track, then just start again. This spiritual practice is not to add one more pressure to your life. This is an invitation to engage with God—an invitation you can accept again and again!

REFLECT

At the end of your song prayer listening time for the day, conduct another self-check-in. How are you feeling? After your listening time is concluded, rank your emotional well-being once again on a scale of 1 to 10 where 1 is the lowest and 10 is optimal. Put down any thoughts

God dropped into your mind as you listened, and use the self-reflection questions to help.

Remember, if you do not want to keep track and self-reflect, then you do not have to. God will still work within you to help you thrive in some ways you might expect and in other ways beyond what you imagined through the daily repetitive listening.

REPEAT

NOW GET STARTED!

Today: Select. Reflect. Listen. Reflect.
Tomorrow: Repeat.

May God bless you richly on your daily listening journey!

PART TWO

DAILY LISTENING REFLECTIONS AND JOURNAL

SELECT, REFLECT, LISTEN, REFLECT, REPEAT

1

TWO

When I chose to surrender my own will so I could worship, pray, listen, obey, and follow God's will, I encountered so many surprises. (And you will encounter them, too). It already felt beyond my imagination to be working with Michael Everett at the Creation Lab to birth the *Ascend in Worship* album. After trying out how the recording process would go with the first four songs in February 2006, we had begun gathering about one weekend per month to initiate production of the additional song prayers a few at a time. These would make up the final eleven, which would comprise the entire album.

However, amid these gatherings, already I felt the Holy Spirit's nudge. At first, I ignored it. *Certainly, I am making this up*, I thought. It was as if the Lord was urging me to start a second album of song prayers while I was still deep in creation of the first, and this did not seem to make sense. Goodness! No one besides those of us working in the studio had even heard the as-yet unfinished song prayers from *Ascend in Worship*.

It did not seem normal to start another project so soon. Who knew if anyone would even listen to *Ascend in Worship*? Certainly, God asks us to do many things that do not make sense! Who records a second album before the first is a success? Didn't there need to be followers of the first so we would have listeners for the second? Wasn't that the *practical* way? Wasn't that the way music production was *supposed* to be done? To begin a second album before anyone listened to the songs on the first and the first album had become well-known went against conventional wisdom on so many human levels. Completing just one album as we were doing was already so far beyond anything I could have ever imagined. Two? Unfathomable.

Maybe I enjoy the recording process so much that I am unduly influencing myself to keep going under the guise that it might be God, I considered. Maybe it wasn't God at all…

But I knew His nudges, and I came to firmly believe that this was from Him.

On the way to lunch one Saturday as we were working on the initial tracking of additional song prayers for *Ascend in Worship* in spring 2006, I mustered up the courage to ask the team if they would be willing to work with me again. My whole body was taut, not knowing what they would say. I was still simultaneously super excited and yet also afraid to be working at the studio. My ability to enjoy this gift God had given me was negatively impacted by a constant sense of incompetence mixed with a bad habit of self-deprecating and disqualifying myself.

I was so surprised and thrilled when they all said yes! Their affirmation that I was 'good enough' to continue the work brought hidden tears to my eyes.

"It's all about You. It's not about me. It's all about You.
Take my life in Your hands. It's Yours to command. It's all about You.
I seek Your face. I need to know You. I have learned, I'm not in control.
It's all about You. It's not about me. It's all about You."

—"All About You" *(Walk on Water album)*

DAY 1

DATE: ____________________

SELECT

Before Daily Listening to Song Prayers

Select where on the album you want to begin listening, set the album on shuffle, or move to a different album or playlist.

REFLECT

Before Daily Listening

Circle your current subjective emotional well-being.

One indicates lowest and ten highest.

1 2 3 4 5 6 7 8 9 10

What's going on for you today?

LISTEN

During-Listening Doodle and Coloring Space

REFLECT

After Daily Listening

Circle your current subjective emotional well-being.

One indicates lowest and ten highest.

1 2 3 4 5 6 7 8 9 10

What did you sense or notice?

What did you feel or experience?

What if any thoughts came to mind while listening?

What songs or lyrics stood out?

What is God speaking to you through today's listening? Do you have words for it?

Unto You, O Lord, do I bring my life. (Ps 25:1)

2

NUANCED

The second album—if I would be brave enough to continue to say "Yes" to its development—was not to be an expansion of the first. The song prayers included were to have a nuanced focus. Namely, this additional album was to include song prayers for when life was not going the way you had hoped and prayed it would.

So much of my initial exposure to adoring God had been a simple repetitive proclaiming of how awesome God was no matter what was happening. Indeed, trust in God was to remain constant during all of life's circumstances—because God remains near to us. He was always present, always over all things, and always in control. I understood that because of His sovereignty, I was to go to Him during every life circumstance. My confidence in Him could not exist only when God seemed to be doing whatever I thought He needed to do. My reliance on Him should also remain when what I (or others around me) were experiencing seemed the opposite or just did not make sense.

Yet, I was becoming aware that authentic worship of God also could not be some put-on positivity of pretending all was well (or that I was emotionally fine with whatever was going on) when this was not the case. The song prayers on this second album needed to include those with lyrics that were vulnerable in how they expressed my confusion, disappointment, impatience and even grief!

It's not as if God did not know how I felt. He always expected me to be forthright with Him! Even Jesus did not pretend He was doing fine emotionally when He was not. I thought of His grief at the death of His friend, Lazarus, and the emotional stress He suffered in anticipation of His torture and murder, which was so great that His physical body sweat blood. The lyrics for these song prayers needed to be transparent, even while continuing to adore God for who He is.

Let's be real. Life includes so many unwanted hardships. When burdens are great, when confusion rages, when discouragement presses down, or when grief stops you in your tracks, you need song prayers that acknowledge this even while you continue to stand in faith. This is not a faith in God to give you His answer your way but a faith that God answers—and, more importantly, never leaves you alone.

Through the lyrics of some of the song prayers on what would become the *Walk on Water* album, God was leading me to express that choice to trust Him simply because He is God, and I am not. Ultimately, He would work out His plan—which would be wonderful—through all things. Even when other people would make harmful or unjust decisions that were destructively impacting, over the long haul none of this could stop God's work on my behalf and on behalf of all of us. The key was coming to see life through the lens of God's eternal, restoring, rectifying perspective.

DAY 2

DATE: ____________________

SELECT

Before Daily Listening to Song Prayers

Select where on the album you want to begin listening, set the album on shuffle, or move to a different album or playlist.

REFLECT

Before Daily Listening

Circle your current subjective emotional well-being.

One indicates lowest and ten highest.

1 2 3 4 5 6 7 8 9 10

What's going on for you today?

LISTEN

During-Listening Doodle and Coloring Space

REFLECT

After Daily Listening

Circle your current subjective emotional well-being.

One indicates lowest and ten highest.

1 2 3 4 5 6 7 8 9 10

What did you sense or notice?

What did you feel or experience?

What if any thoughts came to mind while listening?

What songs or lyrics stood out?

What is God speaking to you through today's listening?
Do you have words for it?

My God, I trust, lean on, rely on *and* am confident in You.
Let me not be put to shame *or* [my hope in You] be disappointed … (Ps. 25:2)

3

RAIN

In February 2006, as the recording progressed for *Ascend in Worship,* Kim Clement, well known in certain Christian circles for his prophetic declarations, released a prophetic word. These were supposedly messages from God to His people. As human beings we hear from God but also hear from Him fallibly, and so prophetic words are not always accurate. Sometimes in our spiritual childlikeness, we do not interpret them accurately. However, this prophetic word contained elements that felt so refreshing to me.

On February 23, my friend, Andrea, forwarded me this written transcript of a message Clement had spoken in January. She highlighted sentences she believed pertained to me:

> For the Spirit of God said, "It shall come to pass that March shall bring about an unusual rain, a rain … so unusual that they shall write about it." And the Spirit of God said, "Let this be a sign to you that the heavens have truly opened … Your praises and your prayers are going to bring about a harvest like you have never seen."

Even though much of the remainder of what Clement declared had to do with God ushering in prosperity and a restoration of seemingly lost promises, this message brought great encouragement to me.

A prayer rose up within me in response:

> Oh, my goodness, Lord. I have a request. God, it would be so cool! If only You would enable it to rain on the days this winter to spring when I go to the studio to record as a sign that I am in Your will (that You will use the music to call and restore Your

people)! Oh, Lord that would be a special gift. I don't need it, but if it could be, it would be wonderful.

God answered my request very specifically. He did not have to, but He did. Northern California indeed did experience unusual rains that winter into spring. Torrential. It especially poured on the Saturdays I was at The Creation Lab. Almost every month that spring, we would gather on a Saturday at The Creation Lab and complete the recording of the initial tracks to three or four more songs, working toward a project total of eleven.

It poured this way every single time we worked on the music. Every time. Weather commentators exhorted people to be careful on the roads due to flooding. Water covered the pavement in a wave. New raindrops splashed into the thick layer of water already present on the road, which had not had time to drain away and gathered like a sea. Drivers were cautioned to stay home and off the road if possible. I drove the one-and-a-half hours carefully to the Creation Lab and carefully back home. I could not stay home! This rain was His accompaniment to the music. I was prudent, though. Far from feeling worried as I drove, I was exhilarated! When Mark was teased by Mike, Brandon, and Larry that he must have brought the odd, profusely rainy weather with him from Colorado, I smiled inside with delight. I knew Who had sent the rain. It almost made me giddy. It strengthened my resolve to continue the recording process. God was confirming that I was in His will and that He would restore others through this work. All thanks be to God!

DAY 3

DATE: ____________________

SELECT

Before Daily Listening to Song Prayers

Select where on the album you want to begin listening,
set the album on shuffle, or move to a different album or playlist.

REFLECT

Before Daily Listening

Circle your current subjective emotional well-being.

One indicates lowest and ten highest.

1 2 3 4 5 6 7 8 9 10

What's going on for you today?

LISTEN

During-Listening Doodle and Coloring Space

REFLECT

After Daily Listening

Circle your current subjective emotional well-being.

One indicates lowest and ten highest.

1 2 3 4 5 6 7 8 9 10

What did you sense or notice?

What did you feel or experience?

What if any thoughts came to mind while listening?

What songs or lyrics stood out?

What is God speaking to you through today's listening?
Do you have words for it?

Yes, let none who trust *and* wait hopefully *and* look for You be put to shame *or* disappointed. (Ps. 25:3a)

4

WATER

The unusual amounts of rain that battered Northern California winter to spring 2006 came like a balm to my soul. They were indeed His confirmation that I was in God's will to develop these albums.

Based on my understanding of certain Scriptures, water (and thus rain) could represent the presence and activity of the Holy Spirit. For instance, in the Old Testament, when the people were aligned with the way of life God had set out for them, they were under His protection and enjoyed His provision. Their harvests were more plentiful, and enemies were kept at bay. But when they de-aligned themselves from His prescribed way of life, their formerly fruitful fields became wastelands where nothing would grow. The difference was the amount of water. When God enabled storms to bring rain, the crops could be planted and flourish. However, no rain meant no water. No water meant no harvest. No harvest meant no food.

Rain was needed to provide sufficient water so that rivers and wells filled, and irrigation ditches could move water into remaining dry spaces. Once the ground was saturated, it also could be plowed and planted. The plants could be nurtured to harvest. The land would be a place of abundant life instead of struggle, starvation, thirst, and death.

In the Bible, verses in John, Ezekiel, and Revelation expand the theme of water and life, seeming to directly and indirectly point to the Holy Spirit. Jesus describes in John 7 how this Living Water would flow into and through those who believe, trust, and rely on Him (vv. 37–39) The Holy Spirit is the Living Water. The Holy Spirit is the Life Giver. St. John also wrote of a river of life shown to him by an angel during the visitation to heaven granted him in his final years. This heavenly river called the water of life flowed out from beneath the throne of God and where the water flowed, there were trees bearing fruit in all seasons

(Rev. 22:2) This seems to match the river the prophet Ezekiel wrote about. This river shown was to him by an angel where the water flowed out from beneath the city and its flow could not be stopped. Where the river flowed there was abundant life. Where it did not, nothing grew. (Ezekiel 47:1–9,11–12)

These passages about spiritual rivers use the image of water to seem to describe how the Holy Spirit will flow into our midst and cause the wasteland of our souls to become fruitful for God. We grow because of the water of the Spirit. We thrive. We are transformed incrementally into His image by this same Spirit as we cooperate with Him. Thus, rainfall to me in 2006 symbolized how the Holy Spirit would touch us and move within us.

In this season of so much rain, the drumbeat of my heart was that these new songs would be infused by the Holy Spirit so that, when completed, they could accomplish His work in listening hearts. The rain to me represented God's outward sign that He was doing precisely that.

DAY 4

DATE: ____________________

SELECT

Before Daily Listening to Song Prayers

Select where on the album you want to begin listening,
set the album on shuffle, or move to a different album or playlist.

REFLECT

Before Daily Listening

Circle your current subjective emotional well-being.

One indicates lowest and ten highest.

1 2 3 4 5 6 7 8 9 10

What's going on for you today?

LISTEN

During-Listening Doodle and Coloring Space

REFLECT

After Daily Listening

Circle your current subjective emotional well-being.

One indicates lowest and ten highest.

1 2 3 4 5 6 7 8 9 10

What did you sense or notice?

What did you feel or experience?

What if any thoughts came to mind while listening?

What songs or lyrics stood out?

What is God speaking to you through today's listening? Do you have words for it?

Show me Your ways, O Lord; teach me Your paths. (Ps. 25:4)

5

MESSAGE

On March 7, 2006, it was raining torrents. As I drove down a flooded, dangerous freeway, the Lord gave me a related prophetic word. I heard words from the Lord begin to drop into my spirit. I knew what to do. With my left hand firmly gripping the steering wheel, I grabbed a nearby pen and paper with my right. Then without looking at the paper (so by feel), I scribbled the words as they were dropping into my mind. My eyes never left the road.

> The March rains prophesied … have begun … Shower after shower comes through soaking and re-soaking the already drenched ground. The symbolism of the rains is for our spiritual spring. A spring season such as this has not been seen, nor will it be seen again for many a year. Seeds long thought dead will be touched by the water of the Lord sent in the rains this spring and finally sprouted. They will grow and flourish this time in a way which … will have produced an abundant, abundant harvest exceeding expectations … Like the crystal-clear water rushing down the gutters in the streets, the living water of God is rushing toward earth from His throne and when the Son/sun touches it, it sparkles like the most precious of diamonds, revealing God's supernatural, spectacular, awesome character.
>
> This is the time of the Lord's breakthrough and the Lord's favor … He indeed has heard the prayers and petitions of His faithful bowed before Him. This is the time we will begin to see undeniably the land turned and restored back to Him by Him … It is not yet time to rejoice, but time to war in violent praise and worship—that the enemy's walls will continue to be broken

down … the Lord's power which is coming in one momentous swoop … will rock the heavens and fill it with sound like a thunderclap. The release of God's power … is like a huge sword coming down in one dramatic whoosh, breaking the enemy's hold, beginning to divide the enemy's armies and disperse them. The purpose of release of God's power is restoration …

Sincerity, sincerity, sincerity. Seeking God alone. Worshipping in His Spirit and His Truth … The Lord seeks intimacy with those who would seek Him and then obediently walk out one step at a time the vision He gives them … that He would be able to speak His secret things to us. He is looking for partners in this mighty release of His restoration power, which is beginning to flow … God is calling. Who will hear?

… God will not be mocked. Do not think you can pray for God to give you what you want and receive it no matter how you are living … God will not tolerate or reward false worship or worship done with the lips but not the heart. Your requests will be ignored. God looks at the heart … A right heart will lead to right actions. God is not looking for perfection but intention, effort, repentance, and perseverance … To receive you must seek Me! … If you want to be in Me, then you are no longer your own but Mine for my purposes. Indeed, as part of the restoration, you yourself will be restored …

Cry out for the rains of March to continue … God is calling His Bride. Will you come?"

DAY 5

DATE: ____________________

SELECT

Before Daily Listening to Song Prayers

Select where on the album you want to begin listening,
set the album on shuffle, or move to a different album or playlist.

REFLECT

Before Daily Listening

Circle your current subjective emotional well-being.

One indicates lowest and ten highest.

1 2 3 4 5 6 7 8 9 10

What's going on for you today?

LISTEN

During-Listening Doodle and Coloring Space

REFLECT

After Daily Listening

Circle your current subjective emotional well-being.

One indicates lowest and ten highest.

1 2 3 4 5 6 7 8 9 10

What did you sense or notice?

What did you feel or experience?

What if any thoughts came to mind while listening?

What songs or lyrics stood out?

What is God speaking to you through today's listening?
Do you have words for it?

Guide me in Your truth *and* faithfulness, for You are the God of my salvation; for You [You only and altogether] do I wait [expectantly] all day long. (Ps. 25:4)

6

SEEDS

The phrase, "Seeds long thought dead will be touched by the water of the Lord sent in the rains this spring and finally sprouted. They will grow and flourish" touched me on the deepest level. It said to me that as I obeyed God to develop these songs, the Holy Spirit was touching them as symbolized by the year's unusual rains. New life would finally spring forth for some people where hope had been lost. The idea was exhilarating and galvanizing.

Every aspect of song production already was put under God by way of our ongoing worship. If as a team we developed the songs by our own skill or power, then the songs ultimately had no worth. Only if God put His power on these song prayers to have His effect on the hearts, minds, and bodies of His listeners would the songs be worth developing.

So many good songs already existed out there. I did not want to be part of adding to the noise of songs developed for purposes other than being vehicles through which God touched His people.

I longed for the Holy Spirit to use these songs that He had purposed and was empowering to cause life to spring forth from seeds long thought dead. I wanted to be part of a more lasting transformation for God's people than what I had often witnessed. For instance, when people attended weekend retreats, clearly many would extol the time they had had away from their everyday lives to focus on their relationship with God. How refreshed they seemed as they returned home. Yet, once the retreat was over, it also seemed that very quickly the effect of the retreat would evaporate, and attendees would find themselves back in the same spiritual condition they had been in before the event—dry.

It was as if daily living as we currently do it resulted in spiritual dryness. It was like living in a spiritual desert, even after going through the motions of daily devotions. Refreshment was vital and needed.

Such Christian events like a retreat seemed to work like a coming to a spiritual oasis; you would come into the green lushness of spiritual refreshing as there was living water through the tangible presence of God there. However, at the end of the retreat, you would return to your personal spiritual desert.

I asked God to change this pattern. Could there be a way to cause people to do more than carry a bucket of living water back to their desert to sustain them in the short term? Could there be a way that people could dig their own spiritual well so their desert could become an oasis of spiritual lushness (and possibility of harvest) for them and others who visited? Now looking back I wonder, is the spiritual practice of daily listening to song prayers and how He responds for each listener individually part of His answer to this long-ago prayer? What do you think?

DAY 6

DATE: ____________________

SELECT

Before Daily Listening to Song Prayers

Select where on the album you want to begin listening,
set the album on shuffle, or move to a different album or playlist.

REFLECT

Before Daily Listening

Circle your current subjective emotional well-being.

One indicates lowest and ten highest.

1 2 3 4 5 6 7 8 9 10

What's going on for you today?

LISTEN

During-Listening Doodle and Coloring Space

REFLECT

<u>After Daily Listening</u>

Circle your current subjective emotional well-being.

One indicates lowest and ten highest.

1 2 3 4 5 6 7 8 9 10

What did you sense or notice?

What did you feel or experience?

What if any thoughts came to mind while listening?

What songs or lyrics stood out?

What is God speaking to you through today's listening?
Do you have words for it?

Remember, O Lord, Your tender mercy and loving-kindness;
for they have ever been from old. (Ps. 25:6)

7

MIRACULOUS

Working at the studio to develop the song prayers was so far beyond anything I could imagine that I felt as if I were living a miracle. My heart was soaring with gratitude to God. When I sought to walk out the 2005 vision for the troops through daily worshiping, praying, listening, and obeying, I would never have thought it would lead to developing His songs at such a high level of professionalism.

The excitement that accompanied the work was visceral and made me giddy alongside a simultaneous and equally intense inner terror of being unmasked as a fraud without having what it took to continue. The song development work was life-giving to me in ways I could not put into words. I did not want this open door to suddenly close again. My heart was soaring with gratitude to God.

It would be a long time before I realized that the terror was unwarranted because how I saw myself was not the truth about me at all. At the advent of working with the studio in whirlwind weekend activity each month—which began with initiating the process of developing the song prayers which would become *Ascend in Worship*—I was not yet even cognizant of the negative thoughts I held against myself. I did not realize how these thoughts diminished my quality of life and my potential to thrive unnecessarily. I thought that these self-condemning, diminutizing, self-deprecating thoughts were the truth of who I was. Why would I consider changing my thoughts when to me they were embedded interiorly as key aspects of my identity?

If you have read my book, *Learning to Love (Not Loathe) Me*, then you know that I was in my forties when I began work at the recording studio. Yet it was first in my sixties that God revealed definitively to me that the thoughts I held against myself were not only unnecessary, but untrue. Additionally, I had not invented these thoughts. They were an outcome of how I had been treated my entire life by some within my family of origin.

I was following where God led to the recording studio and daring to do the work with one objective in mind. I understood this development of the song prayers to be part of God's plan to fulfill the 2005 vision. However, God had more in mind. He used the vision for the troops as the impetus to get me going personally. My worship-pray-listen-obey journey towards getting some of His song prayers "over there", led beyond this to include strides in my own profound inner healing, which I had no inkling I needed. But God did. Thus, before I ever knew, He was calling me forth, not just to help the troops through my obedience, but to heal me (and perhaps you) as well. Miraculous!

DAY 7

DATE: ____________________

SELECT

Before Daily Listening to Song Prayers

Select where on the album you want to begin listening, set the album on shuffle, or move to a different album or playlist.

REFLECT

Before Daily Listening

Circle your current subjective emotional well-being.

One indicates lowest and ten highest.

1 2 3 4 5 6 7 8 9 10

What's going on for you today?

LISTEN

During-Listening Doodle and Coloring Space

REFLECT

After Daily Listening

Circle your current subjective emotional well-being.

One indicates lowest and ten highest.

1 2 3 4 5 6 7 8 9 10

What did you sense or notice?

What did you feel or experience?

What if any thoughts came to mind while listening?

What songs or lyrics stood out?

What is God speaking to you through today's listening?
Do you have words for it?

[Lord] turn to me and be gracious to me, for I am lonely and afflicted. The troubles of my heart are multiplied; bring me out of my distress. (Ps. 25:16-17)

8

CORE

One day a friend said she could hear some inner aching in my songs, a sadness deep in the core. Her statement hurt my heart initially since I did not feel that I was singing with a sense of inner sadness but rather worshiping God with all my heart. In as much as I understood joy, thanksgiving, and awe, these were the emotions with which I was releasing my voice in faith, trust, and obedience into the microphone. I did not want there to be any hint of sadness there!

Yet here already God was showing me kindness. He knew what my conscious mind did not. He knew I had inner emotional wounds from the family-of-origin dysfunction I had experienced since birth. This dysfunction had continued in even more destructive forms into my adulthood. I did walk around with a constant sense of not-good-enough-ness, which caused an even deeper fear of being rejected if I disappointed or did not do enough for others or do what they wanted. That sense of being inherently inadequate had always been there. I did not realize that this was a feeling I could not base on fact because of the innate *enough-ness* with which God made each person. It would be years before God revealed to me that these thoughts around which I had built my identity were not fact but mere thoughts that had grown strong in me as a result of being emotionally mistreated over a long period of time.

Here I was on this path of excitement to develop these song prayers because I loved helping people. I found my value in this, even though my value would never be based on what I did. God had made me with infinite value as I was and by just *being*, that value remained and would always be intact. No action or inaction could change this fact. Yet God had given me this assignment, and it would eventually connect me to you in ways that I continue to consider thrilling!

God is about a greater work, though—the work He sees as the most important—to restore your soul. He wants to restore you to your inner core to the wholeness for which He designed you.

In Scripture, the prophet Ezekiel is given a vision of a valley filled with dry bones, separated and strewn about (Ezek 37). The Spirit of the Lord tells Ezekiel to prophesy over the bones that a breath of new life would come into them from God. The bones are reconstructed and receive new life.

We can draw several meaningful insights from this section of Scripture. I felt as if I was in that valley of dry bones and did not realize it. I was living the life that society set out as 'successful' and purported as the path toward well-being and overall thriving. Yet I was so dried out and lifeless.

No more.

Now, I speak the verses out over you as a prayer and feel convinced that as you seek God, choose to trust Him, seek to listen to Him, and choose to obey, that He will rebuild you and your life in a way that you feel it in your very spiritual bones. You will become satisfied finally like a well-watered garden.

"Thus says the Lord God to these bones, 'Behold, I will make breath enter you so that you may come to life.
I will put sinews on you, make flesh grow back on you, cover you with skin, and I will put breath in you so that you may come alive; and you will know that I am the Lord'"
(Ezek 37:5–6).

DAY 8

DATE: ____________________

SELECT

Before Daily Listening to Song Prayers

Select where on the album you want to begin listening, set the album on shuffle, or move to a different album or playlist.

REFLECT

Before Daily Listening

Circle your current subjective emotional well-being.

One indicates lowest and ten highest.

1 2 3 4 5 6 7 8 9 10

What's going on for you today?

LISTEN

During-Listening Doodle and Coloring Space

REFLECT

After Daily Listening

Circle your current subjective emotional well-being.

One indicates lowest and ten highest.

1 2 3 4 5 6 7 8 9 10

What did you sense or notice?

What did you feel or experience?

What if any thoughts came to mind while listening?

What songs or lyrics stood out?

What is God speaking to you through today's listening?
Do you have words for it?

Hear the voice of my supplication as I cry to You for help, as I lift up my hands toward Your innermost sanctuary (the Holy of Holies) (Ps. 28:2)

9

KIND

I did not share about my core, mostly subconscious, sadness that I struggled with for you to feel sorry for me or think I am painting myself as some sort of victim. Most of us will be victimized in our lives in some way. I think it is part of the human experience for too many of us. My identity is not linked, though, to victimhood. Instead, I highlight here what was going on inside of me because it is a large, beautiful part of the story. I did not know I had need of inner healing. How I felt deep in my core was my identity at that time. I could not remember a time when that feeling was not there. Therefore, I believed that my sense of inadequateness was fact. You could not tell me differently because it was how I felt.

Since the mistreatment that caused me to draw these false conclusions about myself was all I had ever known, I had no way to recognize the impact on me of how I was being treated. Additionally, emotional abuse is not always loud, obnoxious, and obvious. Often it does not have to include yelling but centers on insidious, destructive methods of manipulation and control, which you may even be told are love. (Trust me, they are not.)

Here is yet one more of the wonders of how God works. He loved me too much to leave me in my downtrodden mess of thoughts against myself, which He knew were lies. He did have an assignment for me to help others. He knew with this assignment that He could begin to draw me out of myself. He recognized that I would step out in faith in order to help others but probably not to help myself (especially when I had no idea that I needed the help).

Through development of the song prayers day by day and year by year, I engaged with the music and worshipped God constantly. The more I did, the more He changed my heart. He altered the way I saw myself and my life, first by having me begin to look at Him constantly through the song prayer lyrics. As I got to know Him better, He began to work on my heart, causing me to begin to become aware of the emotional wounds that so drastically impacted my daily well-being. That core inner sadness, which I had denied when my friend sensed it, became undeniable!

Because I was willing to follow God (through a process of worship, pray, listen, and obey), He led me to a place emotionally where He could reveal to me that I hated myself. What a surprise! Truly … I had had no idea. Then He went about the work of layer by layer exposing why and how I had come to think this way. Then He provided His remedy so I could heal.

He brought me from a place of feeling self-diminished to a place of self-acceptance. Ultimately, He provided a miraculous step of healing to a place of appropriate self-love. If you have read my book, *Learning to Love (Not Loathe) Me,* then you know the amazing details of this story! Yet, this much bears repeating here: if you will choose to spend time with God by way of spiritual practices such as listening to song prayers daily, He will uncover where the enemy has held you mentally captive as well. He will heal and set free. Worship Him. Pray. Listen and obey. His path for you will be simultaneously arduous, glorious, and worth every step.

By the way, the friend who told me she sensed an inner sadness in my music also believed this was temporary. Somehow God's Spirit would heal. She was right.

DAY 9

DATE: ____________________

SELECT

Before Daily Listening to Song Prayers

Select where on the album you want to begin listening,
set the album on shuffle, or move to a different album or playlist.

REFLECT

Before Daily Listening

Circle your current subjective emotional well-being.

One indicates lowest and ten highest.

1 2 3 4 5 6 7 8 9 10

What's going on for you today?

LISTEN

During-Listening Doodle and Coloring Space

REFLECT

After Daily Listening

Circle your current subjective emotional well-being.

One indicates lowest and ten highest.

1 2 3 4 5 6 7 8 9 10

What did you sense or notice?

What did you feel or experience?

What if any thoughts came to mind while listening?

What songs or lyrics stood out?

What is God speaking to you through today's listening?
Do you have words for it?

Therefore, is my spirit overwhelmed *and* faints within me [wrapped in gloom]; my heart within my bosom grows numb. (Ps. 143:4)

10

TRANSPARENT

Even though I was finally in a season of action, I still remained in a season of waiting. I had concurrent joy of doing this new work for God and lament over what had not yet come to pass. Have you experienced seasons of life like this, too? It's not like you are ungrateful, but you are so excited or ready for life to be different that you are like a horse chomping at the bit. Yet you do not control the speed at which anything unfolds or how it unfolds. In fact, you control nothing except whether you assent to what God wants to do or fight against it. (The fighting is unproductive and produces negative results.)

Driving back and forth on errands while the children were at school one day in spring 2006, I felt a new song rising up:

> Your timing's not mine, but Your timing is perfect. I wait in joyful hope what You promise You provide. I rejoice in my King, my Savior, and Redeemer. I walk not by sight but by faith in who You are. Hosanna, hosanna, hosanna, my King. Bow before You, adore You, hosanna, my King!

I was in the middle of working through the initial recording process for *Ascend in Worship.* This definitely was not a song prayer that felt right for that album, but I also knew this newest song prayer was important.

This was the second song that spring that had dropped into my mind fully formed with melody and lyrics while I was working on the *Ascend in Worship* album where I sensed a priority in getting the song produced yet it did not fit the current album. The Holy Spirit's urging to write "Your Timing" along with "The Answer was No" that spring was one more confirmation that God wanted tracking to move forward for the second album, *Walk on Water.*

The more time I spent with God and the closer I got to Him, the easier it was to just pour out my heart to Him. Isn't this the way David and the other psalmists had carried out their song (psalm) writing assignments?

The lyrics to "The Answer Was No" began to embody that which I was coming to understand. We could worship God in all circumstances, but it was most helpful if our words changed to reflect what was really going on inside.

"I have prayed till my knees are aching. I have prayed
for what I sought best. Persevering and travailing.
Giving Your throne no rest. Now I have Your answer.
Father God it's not what I sought. Yet, I know You are Sovereign.
You know something I do not. The answer was no, still I worship You.
The answer was no, lift my hands to You, the answer was no
yet I still worship you. I cry and praise You anyway.
Give me strength Lord, for I trust in You."

DAY 10

DATE: ____________________

SELECT

Before Daily Listening to Song Prayers

Select where on the album you want to begin listening,
set the album on shuffle, or move to a different album or playlist.

REFLECT

Before Daily Listening

Circle your current subjective emotional well-being.

One indicates lowest and ten highest.

1 2 3 4 5 6 7 8 9 10

What's going on for you today?

LISTEN

During-Listening Doodle and Coloring Space

REFLECT

After Daily Listening

Circle your current subjective emotional well-being.

One indicates lowest and ten highest.

1 2 3 4 5 6 7 8 9 10

What did you sense or notice?

What did you feel or experience?

What if any thoughts came to mind while listening?

What songs or lyrics stood out?

What is God speaking to you through today's listening?
Do you have words for it?

I remember the days of old; I meditate on all Your doing;
I ponder the works of your hands. (Ps. 143:5)

11

POW

Ever since beginning work at The Creation Lab, I spent hours daily studying the Bible to learn whether Scripture validated what I believed God had shown me about worship when He spoke to me during the open-eye vision of troops marching in a desert in February 2005. The message He conveyed had been something like, "If you will get some of the new worship songs and 'Stand Up' over there, I will be their covering. I will hem them in before and behind. I will be the banner over them and shine my light in the dark places so that the enemy is more easily found." The vision had occurred during a time when thousands of actual troops were deployed in the Global War on Terror to the desert regions of the Middle East. What did God promise if we chose to worship Him? What role did song prayers play in the biblical narratives?

What I found in Scripture seemed to validate the vision. There was something about worshiping God, when people turned their attention toward Him using songs and extolling Him with authentic hearts. In these times, God seemed to interact in response. It's not as if it was a guaranteed reciprocity or as if those worshiping Him could control how He responded or manipulate Him to respond in the way they thought was best. On the contrary, the whole idea of worshiping God in song was to adore Him without asking for anything. He was paid homage because He is God. He was worshipped without expectation of anything in return. Yet, there was this "pow" of His power with which He seemed to interact with the people in response.

You cannot imagine how God intervenes when you worship. Nor can you fathom in advance what the effect of His power coming to your aid is like. When God steps in, the outcome and effect is often beyond what you can fathom.

Worship is prayer because prayer is just another way of saying you are seeking to communicate with God. I have come to believe that worship is one of the most powerful types of prayer because it puts you in your proper position under God. By your worship you demonstrate that your trust in Him is greater than your fear of everything else.

You have only so much time. You can only spend each moment one way. To invest a moment that you have worshipping Him is a choice. You could have spent the time paying attention to your concerns (as if you had any power without His to resolve them). You could have invested the time panicking or becoming so upset that you can only grovel or focus on yourself. Instead, you chose to turn toward God, no matter what is going on, and there you remind Him who He is, what He has done, and how He promises to be. You revel in Him. It is a sacrifice of praise to choose to adore Him versus panicking or begging for the result you want, and so often He responds with what He knows needs to be done. *Pow!*

DAY 11

DATE: ____________________

SELECT

Before Daily Listening to Song Prayers

Select where on the album you want to begin listening,
set the album on shuffle, or move to a different album or playlist.

REFLECT

Before Daily Listening

Circle your current subjective emotional well-being.

One indicates lowest and ten highest.

1 2 3 4 5 6 7 8 9 10

What's going on for you today?

LISTEN

During-Listening Doodle and Coloring Space

REFLECT

<u>After Daily Listening</u>

Circle your current subjective emotional well-being.

One indicates lowest and ten highest.

1 2 3 4 5 6 7 8 9 10

What did you sense or notice?

What did you feel or experience?

What if any thoughts came to mind while listening?

What songs or lyrics stood out?

What is God speaking to you through today's listening?
Do you have words for it?

I spread forth my hands to You; my soul thirsts after You like a thirsty land [for water]. (Psalm 143:6)

12

STRATEGY

One of my favorite Bible stories is the story of King Jehoshaphat and the people of Israel in 2 Chronicles 20. Three enemy armies were coming against them. Jehoshaphat knew that only God could help, so He called the people together to fast. He declared a "remembering prayer" (reference *Ascend in Worship Daily Listening Companion*) to God. He declared a list of many of the ways God had been faithful to help His people through the generations as all the people stood with Him before the Lord. In other words, their attention was turned toward Him. They were listening and expectant of some type of response. Jehoshaphat closed the prayer by remembering to God their current need and asking Him to help them again.

Jehoshaphat believed that God speaks to us, and sometimes this means He speaks through people. The Spirit of the Lord came upon one of those present following the king's prayer, and he declared a prophetic message:

> Listen carefully all [you people of] Judah, and you inhabitants of Jerusalem, and King Jehoshaphat. The LORD says this to you. "Be not afraid or dismayed at this great multitude, for the battle is not yours, but God's. Go down against them tomorrow … You *need* not fight this *battle*; take your positions, stand and witness the salvation of the LORD who is with you, O Judah and Jerusalem. Do not fear or be dismayed; tomorrow go out against them, for the LORD is with you" (2 Chron 20:15–17).

Jehoshaphat bowed before God, and the people fell down before Him, worshiping. They believed that this message was indeed from God, and some began to praise and adore Him loudly.

The following morning, the king and the people gathered to go toward the battle. King Jehoshaphat exhorted the people to believe and trust in the Lord their God. In this way He would take care of them.

Next, King Jehoshaphat ordered the singers, who (as priests) regularly sang before the Lord as a worshipful offering to go out before the army. They were to lead the way, while praising and giving thanks to God because "His mercy *and* lovingkindness endure forever" (2 Chron 20:21). As they began singing and praising, God himself set ambushes against all three of the enemy armies, and they were defeated before Jehoshaphat's army reached them.

Once the army arrived, they experienced only the destroyed enemy armies and dead bodies strewn around. The king and the people had believed the message was from God. No matter how crazy the message may have seemed in light of the seemingly undefeatable united enemy coming against them, they chose to trust God, and as an expression of that trust, they worshiped Him. In fact, singers led the way into battle instead of soldiers. Consider this for a moment. What does it speak to you?

DAY 12

DATE: ____________________

SELECT

Before Daily Listening to Song Prayers

Select where on the album you want to begin listening, set the album on shuffle, or move to a different album or playlist.

REFLECT

Before Daily Listening

Circle your current subjective emotional well-being.

One indicates lowest and ten highest.

1 2 3 4 5 6 7 8 9 10

What's going on for you today?

LISTEN

During-Listening Doodle and Coloring Space

REFLECT

After Daily Listening

Circle your current subjective emotional well-being.

One indicates lowest and ten highest.

1 2 3 4 5 6 7 8 9 10

What did you sense or notice?

What did you feel or experience?

What if any thoughts came to mind while listening?

What songs or lyrics stood out?

What is God speaking to you through today's listening?
Do you have words for it?

Cause me to hear Your loving-kindness in the morning for on You do I lean *and* in You do I trust. Cause me to know the way wherein I should walk, for I lift up my inner self to You. (Ps. 143:8)

13

REJOICE

Of course, just because you choose to worship and know that God promises to somehow respond through interaction with you and your circumstances does not guarantee an outcome like the one you thought you wanted. Have we talked about the absolute necessity of free will for human beings yet?

It is the existence of free will—which God has given to every human being—that complicates life and enables evil to seem as if it sometimes wins. (Short-term evil does seem to win battles because evil choices can have extraordinarily evil effects. In the end, though, only God and His way of love remains, and it is precisely His way of love that necessitates free will as a prerequisite.

Our life assignment is to learn to love like Jesus. This Son gave us the perfect representation of the nature of God's love. Love God, love self, and love others. This is the message Jesus gave when He was asked to define the Greatest Commandment. Love running rightly between us and God, and between us and others results in a way of life that emulates God. When we love as God would, what all the commandments and prophets spoke of is fulfilled. Seeking to love like God elevates us to greater intimacy with Him. We become more like Him. The goal of life is this progressive transformation.

However, we cannot love when we do not choose to love. Authentic love cannot be forced or coerced. Love must be chosen to be love the way God loves. Therefore, the risk is always present that human beings will choose the opposite of loving God's way—and they do.

It can seem confusing to consider the sovereign, almighty nature of God and yet contend with the reality that evil remains for now. It helps to remember that your temporary life represents a season of choice and a time of decision. Will you choose to seek not just to believe in God but to live as a follower of Jesus who lived as the perfect representation of the love of God? Love. Nothing less.

Life here will contain struggle, requiring even more the importance of leaning into God. He is the only One who can make the seemingly impossible possible. His plan may not mirror what you wanted, but His long-term view is always better than ours, even as there is unwanted suffering and heart-sorrow along the way.

One morning driving home after dropping my husband at the airport for a business trip, my mind was overflowing with all that could really use God's help. I wanted to worry. I was tempted to feel sorry for myself and pout. But then I remembered. God is not unaware. I could praise Him. I really could. This would be my expression of trust. "Hey, God, I don't need to beg or plead for anything because, You've got this!"

I will praise Your name, I will rejoice. I will praise Your name,
I will rejoice. I will praise Your name to the heavens every day.
I will rejoice. For You are God. Yes, You are God.
You are the only One who can. For You are God. Yes, You are God.
You are the only One who can.

—"I Will Rejoice" *(Walk on Water album)*

DAY 13

DATE: ____________________

SELECT

Before Daily Listening to Song Prayers

Select where on the album you want to begin listening,
set the album on shuffle, or move to a different album or playlist.

REFLECT

Before Daily Listening

Circle your current subjective emotional well-being.

One indicates lowest and ten highest.

1 2 3 4 5 6 7 8 9 10

What's going on for you today?

LISTEN

During-Listening Doodle and Coloring Space

REFLECT

After Daily Listening

Circle your current subjective emotional well-being.

One indicates lowest and ten highest.

1 2 3 4 5 6 7 8 9 10

What did you sense or notice?

What did you feel or experience?

What if any thoughts came to mind while listening?

What songs or lyrics stood out?

What is God speaking to you through today's listening?
Do you have words for it?

The Lord is my Strength and my [impenetrable] Shield; my heart trusts in, relies on, *and* confidently leans on Him, and I am helped (Ps. 28:7a)

14

WORRY

During 2006, the Lord was also highlighting the concept of worry to me. Worry seemed almost a cultural phenomenon. There was an as if unspoken rule that if you did not worry, then you did not care.

Yet this is not what Jesus says. In the Gospels of Luke and Matthew, Jesus is clear: Do not worry. Do not be anxious.

> Therefore I tell you, stop being worried or anxious (perpetually uneasy, distracted) about your life, as to what you will eat or what you will drink; nor about your body, as to what you will wear. Is life not more than food, and the body more than clothing? Look at the birds of the air; they neither sow [seed] nor reap [the harvest] nor gather [the crops] into barns, and yet your heavenly Father keeps feeding them. Are you not worth much more than they? And who of you by worrying can add one [l]hour to [the length of] his life? … Therefore do not worry or be anxious (perpetually uneasy, distracted), saying, "What are we going to eat?" or "What are we going to drink?" or "What are we going to wear?" For the [pagan] Gentiles eagerly seek all these things; [but do not worry,] for your heavenly Father knows that you need them. But first and most importantly seek (aim at, strive after) His kingdom and His righteousness [His way of doing and being right—the attitude and character of God], and all these things will be given to you also (Matt 6:25–27, 31–33).

The capstone is the final verse in Matthew 6:34, which says, "So do not worry about tomorrow; for tomorrow will worry about itself. Each day has enough trouble of its own."

I kept re-reading this. Do ... not ... worry. Yet, everyone I knew worried and thought it was required. If worrying was a habit that Jesus called us to change, with what were we to replace the activity of worrying? I went from Scripture to Scripture each day to gain clarity regarding what Jesus proposed instead of worry. Oh, my goodness, there will be troubles, but *do not* worry!

The more I searched the Bible, the clearer it became that the antidote to worry is the fear of the Lord, which results in an abject trust in Him. I remembered Peter and the others in the boat in the middle of the Sea of Galilee as Jesus came walking on top of the water to join them. Oh, how they must have trembled when they saw Him!

Then Jesus calls Peter to walk on water toward Him. Peter steps out onto the waves but then sinks because He loses view of Jesus. The answer to worry is to trust God: "Trust in the Lord with all your heart and lean not on your own understanding. In all your ways acknowledge Him and He will make your paths straight" (Prov 3:5–6). The answer is to keep looking at God, remembering how life really is, yet still trusting Him. The answer is to surrender your will and let Him be in charge. God Most High will grab hold of your hand and help you walk with Him on top of the water in the midst of all storms.

"Walk on water, straight into your arms. You will keep me safe,
no matter what the storm. Walk on water, eyes on Your gaze.
I will trust in You for who You are."

—"Walk on Water" *(Walk on Water album)*

DAY 14

DATE: ____________________

SELECT

Before Daily Listening to Song Prayers

Select where on the album you want to begin listening,
set the album on shuffle, or move to a different album or playlist.

REFLECT

Before Daily Listening

Circle your current subjective emotional well-being.

One indicates lowest and ten highest.

1 2 3 4 5 6 7 8 9 10

What's going on for you today?

LISTEN

During-Listening Doodle and Coloring Space

smile

REFLECT

After Daily Listening

Circle your current subjective emotional well-being.

One indicates lowest and ten highest.

1 2 3 4 5 6 7 8 9 10

What did you sense or notice?

What did you feel or experience?

What if any thoughts came to mind while listening?

What songs or lyrics stood out?

What is God speaking to you through today's listening?
Do you have words for it?

… my heart greatly rejoices, and with my song I will praise Him. (Ps. 28:7b)

15

GRACE

Spring 2006 moved into summer. The *Ascend in Worship* album was complete. It had been mixed in Turlock by Michael Everett and mastered in Nashville. Arrangements had been made for its manufacture into CDs. Michael Everett had travelled to Yosemite at summer's onset to take photos for the album cover and lyric booklet. The late spring greens, lush waterfalls and profusion of resident mosquitos were evidence of the spring's unusual rains during the album's development.

The first version of "Stand Up" was also complete and had been reproduced on CDs. The title of this initial version of the song was "We Will Fight for Freedom," which echoed the first line of the song.

I could barely breathe waiting to receive the first copies of *Ascend in Worship*. Yes, *Walk on Water* was also in production, which was thrilling, but once *Ascend in Worship* arrived and was coupled with "We Will Fight for Freedom," it would represent the first time since February 2005 that I could ship the music to the troops 'over there.' This would lead to fulfillment of the vision, wouldn't it?

But what now? Where did it go from here? What would happen when some of the CDs were delivered 'over there' as He had instructed? Would the troops listen to the songs? Would they worship Him with the song prayers? (Did they understand what worshiping God was?) What would God do in response to their arrival? Instead of feeling as though I was almost to the point of mission accomplished, it seemed I had only just begun.

My sister reached out one day to let me know there was a woman she believed I was supposed to meet. She was a mother in the same homeschool group as my sister, her husband, and family. The woman's name was Grace. My sister provided the contact information and urged me to reach out.

I thought about how God had connected me to Michael Everett and several others. This seemed to be a way that God connected me with people when He wanted connection between us, so I called her. As I recollect, Grace had been expecting my call.

In the initial minutes of getting to know one another, Grace mentioned that she and her husband, Dean, were worship leaders at a local church. He also worked full-time at a corporation while she homeschooled their four young children. Now that the youngest had turned two, the Lord had released Grace to begin teaching voice and piano again. For the time being, though, she was only to instruct those involved in the ministry of worship.

I was speechless. I had been talking to God about a vocal coach. Here I was singing into a microphone, yet the only instruction I had had was about thirty years ago in high school. I began travelling two hours round trip to Elk Grove where Grace and her family lived weekly. More than helping my voice, Grace understood the assignment God had given me. In many Holy Spirit-led discussions over many years, she helped me steward my voice, and still does.

DAY 15

DATE: ____________________

SELECT

Before Daily Listening to Song Prayers

Select where on the album you want to begin listening, set the album on shuffle, or move to a different album or playlist.

REFLECT

Before Daily Listening

Circle your current subjective emotional well-being.

One indicates lowest and ten highest.

1 2 3 4 5 6 7 8 9 10

What's going on for you today?

LISTEN

During-Listening Doodle and Coloring Space

REFLECT

After Daily Listening

Circle your current subjective emotional well-being.

One indicates lowest and ten highest.

1 2 3 4 5 6 7 8 9 10

What did you sense or notice?

What did you feel or experience?

What if any thoughts came to mind while listening?

What songs or lyrics stood out?

What is God speaking to you through today's listening?
Do you have words for it?

Lean on, trust in *and* be confident in the Lord with all your heart *and* mind and do not rely on your own insight or understanding. (Prov. 3:5)

16

INVITATION

September 2006 arrived, and the CDs were following a standard month or more process to manufacture and ship across the country back to Turlock. For me, the waiting continued to feel challenging. (I worshiped to "Your Timing" often to better come to rest in God and receive His peace in the waiting.)

Only with hindsight could I more clearly recognize how God was putting so much into place for what He wanted in the years ahead. My main job that fall was to trust Him, which manifested in continuing to pursue a lifestyle of worship, and then to pray, listen to Him, and obey.

A cherished friend, who had been part of the initial weeks in Andrea's autumn 2003 Bible study, knew how the others had prayed for me to hear new worship songs on February 18, 2004. She knew about the vision to get music to the troops in February 2005, and she was a powerful, faithful intercessor for me as I began working with The Creation Lab to develop the album, *Ascend in Worship.* This friend and her husband at that time, sent me an invitation to a mini conference/retreat called "Salt and Light." It was going to be hosted by a famous pastor named Jack Hayford from Southern California and a university he had recently founded, called The King's University.

I knew nothing about the university and had only heard brief snippets from some of Pastor Hayford's many teaching radio programs. I liked what I had heard but knew no more about the man.

My friends were well acquainted with Jack Hayford's ministry and the university. I felt the Holy Spirit nudge me to respond affirmatively when I received their invitation, but I was hesitant. Generally, I stayed home with my family on weekends. Normal weekend happenings included things like a date lunch my husband and I would often enjoy together along with shuttling the children back and forth to their activities.

I knew Holy Spirit was pointing me toward attendance, though, and His insistence felt strong. I was to break our norm and attend the Salt and Light weekend (whatever that was).

On the first evening of the event, as I entered the hotel and approached the banquet room where dinner would be served, I had no idea that this weekend would lead to connections, community, education and confirmations which would further my mission for God in a way that spanned decades. Yet, this is how obedience to God works. Only He knows fully why He is asking you to do what you are sensing. You can ignore Him, or you can take His hand and plunge into that which does not necessarily make sense until He amazes you with what He planned from before the beginning as an outcome of your simple act of obedience.

DAY 16

DATE: ____________________

SELECT

Before Daily Listening to Song Prayers

Select where on the album you want to begin listening,
set the album on shuffle, or move to a different album or playlist.

REFLECT

Before Daily Listening

Circle your current subjective emotional well-being.

One indicates lowest and ten highest.

1 2 3 4 5 6 7 8 9 10

What's going on for you today?

LISTEN

During-Listening Doodle and Coloring Space

REFLECT

After Daily Listening

Circle your current subjective emotional well-being.

One indicates lowest and ten highest.

1 2 3 4 5 6 7 8 9 10

What did you sense or notice?

What did you feel or experience?

What if any thoughts came to mind while listening?

What songs or lyrics stood out?

What is God speaking to you through today's listening?
Do you have words for it?

In all your ways acknowledge Him, and He will direct *and* make straight *and* plain your path. (Prov. 3:6)

17

PEOPLE

When I entered the banquet room of the hotel, my attention went to a tall, slender, elegant woman standing at the door. She was greeting the guests as they entered. I stopped cold. It couldn't be, could it? How did this even make sense? The woman was my friend, Tamara, who had led our weekly Moms in Prayer meeting at the elementary school where both of our children had attended. At the end of the school year a number of years before, she had asked me to pray for her. Her husband was taking a new job in Southern California. Would I cover them in prayer as she and her family made this transition? I responded that I would, and I did. I had continued to pray for Tamara and her family as Holy Spirit brought them to mind all the years since they had left, leading up to this night.

In what I could only understand as a God-incidence, here she was at the same event where I was in Northern California. As it turned out, the job her husband had taken and for which I had been praying was as president of The King's University. So, of course, as his wife, Tamara was there greeting guests who were current donors and potential future donors and students.

Honestly, I was thrilled to see her. It had been sad that we had not stayed in touch. We had a lot of catching up to do! We exchanged contact information. That would be for another day.

Shortly after I found my assigned table, the worship music began. Before anything else, we were going to worship Jesus.

As the worship ascended from the musicians, vocalists, and those of us in attendance, a vibration of what I had come to recognize as the Holy Spirit filled the room. Though I cannot recall the exact flow of the evening, Jack Hayford was introduced along with his worship leader, Sy

Goraieb. As they spoke of their work in the area of worship over the past thirty to forty years, I was stunned. I had found my people.

For almost a year I had been voraciously studying the Scriptures looking for evidence of what God promises when we worship. Yet for decades already, Jack Hayford had been writing and teaching on exactly what I was trying to learn and discern. Hayford gave each of us a copy of one of his books. I gobbled in up in short order and highlighted almost everything. What I thought I had found in Scripture about worship was what Hayford had already been teaching for a long time.

I wanted to be around Pastor Jack and the others affiliated with his church and university more. The Holy Spirit kindled a deep yearning within me to get involved, but it would be years yet before He finally released me to attend The King's.

DAY 17

DATE: ____________________

SELECT

Before Daily Listening to Song Prayers

Select where on the album you want to begin listening,
set the album on shuffle, or move to a different album or playlist.

REFLECT

Before Daily Listening

Circle your current subjective emotional well-being.

One indicates lowest and ten highest.

1 2 3 4 5 6 7 8 9 10

What's going on for you today?

LISTEN

During-Listening Doodle and Coloring Space

REFLECT

After Daily Listening

Circle your current subjective emotional well-being.

One indicates lowest and ten highest.

1 2 3 4 5 6 7 8 9 10

What did you sense or notice?

What did you feel or experience?

What if any thoughts came to mind while listening?

What songs or lyrics stood out?

What is God speaking to you through today's listening?
Do you have words for it?

He heals the brokenhearted and binds up their wounds [curing their pains and their sorrows]. (Ps. 147:3)

18

MISSIONARY

At the beginning of October 2006, I received word that the *Ascend in Worship* CDs had shipped! They were finally on their way from the eastern USA to Turlock, California, expected to arrive soon, but that could mean days to a week or more. No one could predict the day, but Mike would let me know when they arrived.

My new friend, Grace, who had been helping me with my song prayer vocals, wanted some of her people she knew to pray over me before the CDs came. Her friend, Marie, traveled as with a prayer missionary named Rhonda as one of her intercessors. Rhonda was also an author and wanted others to know Jesus on a more intimate level to help change their lives for the better.

As I waited for word that the CDs had arrived, Marie and Rhonda happened to be travelling and holding meetings in Northern California. Grace reached out to the women to see if they were open to praying over me before I took possession of the CDs. They were.

Grace and I brainstormed when and where I might be able to fit into my schedule travelling to where the women were ministering. Honestly, there was only one time and location that looked possibile. It was midday on a weekday. This location was the longest drive from our home. Attending would be somewhat of a strain. I would have to drop the children at school, drive to the gathering, participate, receive prayer, and get back into our area before the children got out of school. Still, the Holy Spirit's nudge to attend was strong.

As it turned out, the meeting was at a woman's home in Turlock, California. What?! The location almost took my breath away. Could this be a God setup? It felt it could be. I mean, wouldn't it be amazing if I got the call from Mike while I was there?! I didn't want to get my hopes up, though. I was just happy to obey and attend the gathering to receive prayer at the end. Try as I might, it just kept feeling as though God had set things up to have me in Turlock already when the CDs arrived.

The gathering was wonderful. Rhonda taught and then we all prayed for one another. Per Grace's Holy Spirit nudge, Rhonda and Marie prayed for me, and then I prayed for them.

Just as the prayer time was winding down, my cell phone rang. It was Michael Everett! The boxes of 1,000 *Ascend in Worship* CDs had just been delivered. He had no idea I was already in Turlock. I said I would be there to pick them up in ten minutes.

I wept listening to the album on the way home. Wow … just *wow*! Amazing God! On so many levels … amazing!

DAY 18

DATE: ____________________

SELECT

Before Daily Listening to Song Prayers

Select where on the album you want to begin listening,
set the album on shuffle, or move to a different album or playlist.

REFLECT

Before Daily Listening

Circle your current subjective emotional well-being.

One indicates lowest and ten highest.

1 2 3 4 5 6 7 8 9 10

What's going on for you today?

LISTEN

During-Listening Doodle and Coloring Space

REFLECT

After Daily Listening

Circle your current subjective emotional well-being.

One indicates lowest and ten highest.

1 2 3 4 5 6 7 8 9 10

What did you sense or notice?

What did you feel or experience?

What if any thoughts came to mind while listening?

What songs or lyrics stood out?

What is God speaking to you through today's listening?
Do you have words for it?

The Lord lifts up the humble and downtrodden;
He casts the wicked to the ground. (Ps. 147: 5-6)

19

DECEMBER

Now I finally had the CDs, but I still had few military contacts or even people who might know someone who knew someone else to help provide connections to the service member community. Thus, my journey with this assignment from God had only just begun. God continued to methodically, intentionally put people, organizations, and activities into my life who He wanted to remain.

For instance, around November, I received an email about the establishment of a little prayer room less than two miles from our home that would be similar in structure to the one in the Midwest where Rhonda and Marie were active. I attended their December training for new potential volunteers. Just as I had felt immediately connected to those in Hayford's circle and from the university he had founded, so too was the connection with those who were part of the East Bay Prayer Furnace. Worship and prayer before God was the foundation for everything. All else in life was to flow out from it. Those who were involved were also listening for God's will through the Holy Spirit and seeking to obey with their lives. They were committed to a lifestyle of offering God night and day musical worship based on Scripture and intercession.

Additionally, in December, Grace was invited to lead Christmas worship at a local rural property that the owners had dedicated to God. Grace knew that my heart for worship matched hers. We had also found that God worked beautiful tones through our voices together when we worshiped improvisationally. Grace asked if I would like to co-lead Christmas worship with her at the nearby home of Al and Sue, who often made the large back room available for prayer and worship gathering. I assented, and Grace gave me the assignment of reviewing traditional Christmas carols to see which ones we could use for our worship.

To my surprise, there were few Christmas carols that actually adored God. Many told the story of the birth of a beloved Savior and declared the wonder of how He came to redeem us back to eternal life with God. Others beckoned carolers and listeners to join in believing and choosing to become followers of Jesus. Yet most lyrics did not address God personally. They spoke of Him in the third person. The lyrics simply did not adore.

God needed to be worshiped at Christmas! By having me review so many carols, He planted a longing in me to create song prayers that adored Jesus in light of the gift of His birth at Christmas and all that His birth means for those who believe and seek to follow Him forever.

DAY 19

DATE: ____________________

SELECT

Before Daily Listening to Song Prayers

Select where on the album you want to begin listening, set the album on shuffle, or move to a different album or playlist.

REFLECT

Before Daily Listening

Circle your current subjective emotional well-being.

One indicates lowest and ten highest.

1 2 3 4 5 6 7 8 9 10

What's going on for you today?

LISTEN

During-Listening Doodle and Coloring Space

REFLECT

After Daily Listening

Circle your current subjective emotional well-being.

One indicates lowest and ten highest.

1 2 3 4 5 6 7 8 9 10

What did you sense or notice?

What did you feel or experience?

What if any thoughts came to mind while listening?

What songs or lyrics stood out?

What is God speaking to you through today's listening? Do you have words for it?

I will extol You, my God, O King; and I will bless Your name forever and ever [with grateful, affectionate praise (Ps. 145:1)

20

RE-DO

December 2006 was the first time the song, "Stand Up" was broadcast on a radio program. It was the initial arrangement of the song titled, "We Will Fight for Freedom," drawn from the first line of the first verse. (The name "Stand Up" came from the chorus.) This was exciting!

The radio program had military-related content and was hosted by a man my dad had known while studying at the Naval Academy in the mid-1950s. Dad had graduated but never fully served. He had received an honorable discharge following graduation because he had injured his knee wrestling for a Naval Academy team. Dad's long past years there did not open doors to many contacts for me except for this veteran he knew. After I reached out to the radio host, he agreed to broadcast the song on his program.

A day later, my friend, Andrea, and I met for coffee and discussion after dropping our children at school. Andrea was never known for holding back. She spoke her mind: "You need to do a new version of that patriotic song. It needs to be redone as a rock anthem or something. What you have now will not do."

I cringed. I knew she was right, but I also didn't understand what I was supposed to do with 900 copies of the song arranged and produced like I thought the Holy Spirit had directed me to do: like an old-fashioned Souza march.

Thoughts were running around in my mind as Andrea and I continued our discussion. She showed me a thank you card she had received from one of Queen Elizabeth II's ladies-in-waiting in response to Andrea's gift of a copy of the *Ascend in Worship* album.

This was indeed a little stunning to see! When Andrea, Nicole, and Lori had prayed over me on February 18, 2004 to begin hearing and writing songs that were already being sung in heaven—songs that

God wanted released on the earth—they had also declared that these songs would go around the world. Shortly thereafter, Andrea had been insistent that someday I would have CDs.

I had laughed at her.

But she was right.

I needed to let go of thinking that "We Will Fight for Freedom" with this old-fashioned arrangement was right for the current generation of service members. I did not understand why the Holy Spirit had been so insistent that the song be produced that way, but He had. I realized once again that I didn't need to know. I just needed to surrender my pride, listen again, and go forward in obedience.

Andrea called again once I was home. She had seen something on the television that caused her to think the current Souza-march rendition was for children. That felt right. I agreed. I sat down at my desk to begin researching organizations that provided gifts to military children. I contacted Michael Everett and booked the studio for February 18, 2007 to begin recording a new rock-anthem version of "Stand Up."

DAY 20

DATE: ____________________

SELECT

Before Daily Listening to Song Prayers

Select where on the album you want to begin listening,
set the album on shuffle, or move to a different album or playlist.

REFLECT

Before Daily Listening

Circle your current subjective emotional well-being.

One indicates lowest and ten highest.

1 2 3 4 5 6 7 8 9 10

What's going on for you today?

LISTEN

During-Listening Doodle and Coloring Space

grace

REFLECT

After Daily Listening

Circle your current subjective emotional well-being.

One indicates lowest and ten highest.

1 2 3 4 5 6 7 8 9 10

What did you sense or notice?

What did you feel or experience?

What if any thoughts came to mind while listening?

What songs or lyrics stood out?

What is God speaking to you through today's listening?
Do you have words for it?

Great is our Lord and of great power; His understanding is inexhaustible *and* boundless. (Ps. 147:5)

21

FIRST

In early 2007, a friend offered to get some of my albums to deployed troops in Afghanistan. I was thrilled. She would need about thirty sets of whatever I wanted to give her by afternoon to be packed in her husband's suitcase. He was a retired NFL player and part of a goodwill group headed to the Middle East around the time of the Pro Bowl to meet with service members.

I felt beyond thrilled. In my heart, I felt as if God had whispered that the CDs were supposed to go to Iraq first, but memory of this blurred with my friend's offer to get the CDs "over there" *any*where.

I scrambled considering how to package the CDs. I decided on what I had at hand: red, white and blue curling ribbon with a little business-card-sized note attached that let the recipient know it was a gift and said a blessing over them. As I giftwrapped each CD set with the ribbons, I prayed for the troops and that the music would accomplish the purpose for which God had designed it.

I rushed the CD sets to my friend, and she made sure they were in the suitcase. However, her husband was the only one in the group whose luggage got lost before their first stop. His luggage was never recovered during the trip, but delivered to him again after he was home. I was incredulous and so disappointed—that is, until I remembered the whisper from the Holy Spirit sometime before. He wanted the CDs to be delivered to service members in Iraq first. He meant what He had communicated.

Meanwhile, outreach to several organizations that sent packages to deployed service members was beginning to bear fruit. One local organization welcomed inclusion of my little red-white-and-blue ribbon-adorned CD packages in their packages. Meanwhile, in our San Ramon home, my husband's cousin was helping us with some renovations. He was an extraordinary general contractor. He popped his head into the drop-down family room where I was preparing the CDs for sending. He also was a Navy veteran. He said there would be others who would want to take part in what I was doing. Had I thought about founding a non-profit? I said I had not but that of course, if I felt God told me to, I would proceed. We talked a little further. One of the stumbling blocks for me were the potential costs of hiring an attorney to draw up the legal documents. He asked me if I would perceive it as a message from God to proceed if he gave me some money toward the attorney.

I was stunned. I did an interior check with God regarding what He thought about this and then responded "yes" to my husband's cousin, Jim. He wrote me a check, and I began to listen for how God wanted me to move forward as I did some online research.

Soon after, while on a walk on Inspiration Hill near our children's home, I asked God for His name for the non-profit. (You cannot register a new non-profit corporation without a name.) As I raised my eyes to a higher hill in the distance, the Lord whispered, "Eagles Nest Foundation," to my heart. I had no idea yet why or what Eagles Nest Foundation would fully entail, but the Lord had given me His name for the organization. Glorious!

DAY 21

DATE: ____________________

SELECT

Before Daily Listening to Song Prayers

Select where on the album you want to begin listening,
set the album on shuffle, or move to a different album or playlist.

REFLECT

Before Daily Listening

Circle your current subjective emotional well-being.

One indicates lowest and ten highest.

1 2 3 4 5 6 7 8 9 10

What's going on for you today?

LISTEN

During-Listening Doodle and Coloring Space

REFLECT

After Daily Listening

Circle your current subjective emotional well-being.

One indicates lowest and ten highest.

1 2 3 4 5 6 7 8 9 10

What did you sense or notice?

What did you feel or experience?

What if any thoughts came to mind while listening?

What songs or lyrics stood out?

What is God speaking to you through today's listening?
Do you have words for it?

Then he showed me the river whose waters give life, sparkling like crystal, flowing out from the throne of God and the Lamb. (Rev. 22:1)

22

NINETY-ONE

Until you have had something happen in your life that seems to violate spiritual principles as you thought you understood them, it can feel tempting to slap another Bible verse or out-of-context explanation onto another person's situation in blindness to what is currently going on. The reasons for this are numerous. Perhaps it feels uncomfortable for you to see another person struggling or even suffering, so you want to placate them with what you hope is a quick fix (when such actions and words generally fix nothing). Perhaps you do not want to face the truth that some aspects of how God operates defy what you thought you understood (given a particular Bible verse), and you don't want to consider that God is not quite that way at all.

For example, I became aware that many military families were praying Psalm 91 over their loved ones. Service members were praying Psalm 91 relying on the verses themselves as assurance, that God would keep them physically and emotionally safe.

Yet deaths on the battlefield and beyond remained a stark reality—even when Psalm 91 and other Scripture had been prayed repeatedly. Had God failed? Had He been unfaithful? Both these questions are valid. (Any questions before God are valid as questioning is part of seeking Him.) Simultaneously, it was important to stop looking for ways to explain away why something bad had happened to someone else.

People do not need a pat answer extracted from Scripture and applied inaccurately. They do not need a trivializing of the loss that comes through hurtful attempts at explanation such as "God's will is best and always good," or "Now your loved one has gained their wings and is in heaven watching over you." (We do not become angels when we die.) What people need is presence and compassion.

So, what were we to do instead when confronted with very real circumstances that did not match how we had believed and hoped God would answer our prayers? Perhaps the better answer lay in confronting the reality that as children of God, some reality remains frustratingly mysterious to us.

We would be uncomfortable. We should embrace our smallness in comparison to the overarching supremacy of God. Instead of trying to explain away what we did not understand, we should continue to pray and seek God more. We could ask Him to reveal a greater understanding of His way with what confused us through Scripture.

We can get comfortable with being uncomfortable. In our lack of complete understanding and in our inability to fix another person's situation, we can simply come alongside them. Instead of minimizing or disregarding the experiences, thoughts, and feelings of others with pat answers that don't hold up when we look underneath, perhaps we can seek to enter their pain and just be present.

Be honest with a person when you do not understand. Weep with them and tell them the truth: that you have no adequate words. In this, we love one another more like Jesus does. (I am still learning how to do this. Are you?)

DAY 22

DATE: ____________________

SELECT

Before Daily Listening to Song Prayers

Select where on the album you want to begin listening,
set the album on shuffle, or move to a different album or playlist.

REFLECT

Before Daily Listening

Circle your current subjective emotional well-being.

One indicates lowest and ten highest.

1 2 3 4 5 6 7 8 9 10

What's going on for you today?

LISTEN

During-Listening Doodle and Coloring Space

REFLECT

After Daily Listening

Circle your current subjective emotional well-being.

One indicates lowest and ten highest.

1 2 3 4 5 6 7 8 9 10

What did you sense or notice?

What did you feel or experience?

What if any thoughts came to mind while listening?

What songs or lyrics stood out?

What is God speaking to you through today's listening?
Do you have words for it?

There shall no longer exist there anything that is accursed (detestable, foul, offensive, impure, hateful, or horrible). But the throne of God and the Lamb shall be in it ... (Rev. 22:3a)

23

UNLESS

In the weeks preceding February 18, 2007, I felt genuinely bothered by the idea of creating this rock anthem arrangement of "Stand Up" without creating a song prayer for those grieving the loss of one or more fallen warriors. Inner resolve rose within me along with that bit of feisty defiance God had given me for those instances. The Holy Spirit knew I needed to stand up to God. I boldly began repeating a message to God in prayer: "Lord, I won't take 'Stand Up' forward to the troops unless you give me a song for those who are suffering with loss from the Global War on Terror."

In the days preceding the recording session during a walk on Inspiration Hill, God dropped a melody and lyrics into my mind in direct response to that prayer. This caused me to tingle all over with His presence and feel overwhelmed at how amazing He was. The song was called, "You Carry Me." Thus, on February 18, we began tracking not only the new arrangement of "Stand Up" but "You Carry Me" as well.

"You Carry Me" became the capstone to the *Walk on Water* album. In fact, another song was removed from the project to make room for it. Now *Walk on Water* felt complete.

The families of fallen warriors as well as others who grieved them were constantly on my mind and heart. (They still are.) In late April 2007, I traveled as a chaperone to Washington, DC with the eighth-grade class of our second daughter. The only other time I had ever been in Washington, DC was on a similar trip with our older daughter two years prior. Before we traveled as a group to Arlington National Cemetery, the Holy Spirit dropped an instruction into my mind. I was to sing "You Carry Me" for the first time outside the recording studio walls when we disembarked the tour bus at Section 60, where some of those who had died in the Global War on Terror were buried.

I wanted to do this to honor those who had died, and prophetically to release the sound of the song over those who were buried there as well as for all the other fallen and for those who grieve for them. However, the idea of singing out loud with a busload of eighth graders, parents, and teachers around was disconcerting.

When we got off the bus at Section 60, I tried to find a private corner to complete the assignment. I was not entirely successful, but I asked God to give me the courage to rise above my self-consciousness and release the song anyway. He helped me, and I sang "You Carry Me" for the first time into the atmosphere. I continue to hold families of fallen warriors and those who grieve with them closely in my heart.

Meanwhile, the Holy Spirit had also nudged me to add troops who could sing for other troops to the new arrangement of "Stand Up." They were to sing with me on the choruses. I really did not know who the Spirit meant or what the make-up of the group was supposed to be. I also had no idea where to find anyone who could do this. My contact with any service members or their families remained quite limited. Nonetheless, I would worship, pray, listen, and obey until He led me to those He had in mind.

DAY 23

DATE: ____________________

SELECT

Before Daily Listening to Song Prayers

Select where on the album you want to begin listening,
set the album on shuffle, or move to a different album or playlist.

REFLECT

Before Daily Listening

Circle your current subjective emotional well-being.

One indicates lowest and ten highest.

1 2 3 4 5 6 7 8 9 10

What's going on for you today?

LISTEN

During-Listening Doodle and Coloring Space

REFLECT

After Daily Listening

Circle your current subjective emotional well-being.

One indicates lowest and ten highest.

1 2 3 4 5 6 7 8 9 10

What did you sense or notice?

What did you feel or experience?

What if any thoughts came to mind while listening?

What songs or lyrics stood out?

What is God speaking to you through today's listening? Do you have words for it?

Then I saw the new sky (heaven) and a new earth for the former sky and the former earth had passed away (vanished) and there no longer existed any seas … (Rev. 21:1)

24

PRE-DAWN

In the Spring of 2007, I still felt deep longings in my soul. I thought these longings could be addressed by God allowing the song prayers to become well known and used by those for whom He intended them as tools to worship Him. I continued to grow in my understanding of what God would do if others worshiped Him. Indeed, He would inhabit their praises and be active in their lives in response. Sometimes He would act in ways that made sense, and sometimes in ways beyond what we could imagine. Other times, it might be in ways people were unaware of until He revealed what He had done. I also longed for the song prayers to become known and utilized on a widespread basis in order to validate that I had heard from God in creating them!

It remained amazing that these albums were being developed to the caliber that they were. I was in constant bowed-down awe for His connection with The Creation Lab and how Michael Everett and the team continued to agree to work with me. We were also becoming friends, which deeply touched my heart.

Yet, I continued to find myself in a season of waiting (and waiting some more) for God to do something with all He was having me create. I did this as I worked to stay courageous and obey what I believed He was dropping into my mind. Waiting is not easy because you cannot see what ultimately will be, and often you have particular hopes linked with particular expectations—especially when you are first learning and growing in God.

I found the waiting difficult even though I trusted and only wanted God's plan and however He desired to unfold it. I was talking to Him regularly (praying) about my longing for more doors to open and more of His effect to take place.

In March 2007, I was invited to the sixth birthday party for Grace and Dean's daughter, Harmony. I stayed overnight with them. That night I left the window of the room I was in open to the refreshing night air. As had happened in every Northern California spring since I could remember, sometime in February or March the birds begin to sing in the dark of 2 a.m. or 3 a.m. It is as if they are already anticipating the spring that has not yet come.

I got out of bed and leaned up toward the window and listened. A new song prayer rose up within me. The birds singing in the dark gave me a picture of how calls us to be. Those birds were confident that spring was coming. It did not enter their consciousness that there was a possibility of no spring. Thus, still in the dark before the dawn, they sang. They lifted their voices and released their song into the atmosphere as a form of praise—rejoicing already in what could not yet be seen. What an example for me. I embraced it!

O teach me to be like the birds of the air.
Teach me to be like the lilies.
To lift up my voice without any care and rejoice,
I know You are there.

—"Before the Dawn" *(Walk on Water album)*

DAY 24

DATE: ____________________

SELECT

Before Daily Listening to Song Prayers

Select where on the album you want to begin listening,
set the album on shuffle, or move to a different album or playlist.

REFLECT

Before Daily Listening

Circle your current subjective emotional well-being.

One indicates lowest and ten highest.

1 2 3 4 5 6 7 8 9 10

What's going on for you today?

LISTEN

During-Listening Doodle and Coloring Space

REFLECT

After Daily Listening

Circle your current subjective emotional well-being.

One indicates lowest and ten highest.

1 2 3 4 5 6 7 8 9 10

What did you sense or notice?

What did you feel or experience?

What if any thoughts came to mind while listening?

What songs or lyrics stood out?

What is God speaking to you through today's listening?
Do you have words for it?

Then I heard a mighty voice from the throne *and* I perceived its distinct words, saying, See! The abode of God is with men, and He will life (encamp, tent) among them ... (Rev 21:3a)

25

BIRTHDAY

It was just so cool (or so I thought) that the Lord led me to schedule the recording day (for troops singing for troops on the choruses of "Stand Up") on my birthday, which was Saturday, May 19, 2007. I did not tell anyone meeting at the studio that it was my birthday. Just being there working on this part of "Stand Up" on that day was the gift.

As usual, it had been an adventure walking out God's will until He revealed what He intended when He asked me to gather troops to sing for troops. This time, the first idea that dropped into my mind was to contact some of the various branches of the military to find out if they had musical resources with an interest to participate. For instance, I reached out to the Naval Academy choirs. No one responded. OK, then, Lord, what next? His next inner prompt was to find someone representing each branch of the military as part of this choir.

I telephoned a nearby Marine Corps base and told the woman who answered that I was looking for a "Soldier" who might be interested in being part of the troops singing for troops choir. Very firmly but politely, she asked me if I was looking for a Solider or a Marine. Oh, my … I was still so new to military communities that I did not have a grasp on basic vocabulary yet. A Marine! I was looking for a Marine!

Little by little, God put together His group of singers. A friend referred a Coastie[1] who was known for his strong, magnificent voice. The Lord sent an Air Force veteran who was a dentist. Grace's father-in-law would be in California from Texas. He was a Navy veteran. Another friend of Grace's came who was a Marine veteran. The father of a deployed Soldier whose son was deployed to Iraq came to sing on

1 Informal term for a member of the Coast Guard

behalf of the Army. His wife accompanied him to be an intercessor, but we encouraged her to sing, too. Grace sang on behalf of future generations of service members, and another woman who came as an intercessor was invited to sing as well on behalf of past generations. Her father had served in the Korean War.

It was an amazing experience to hear all their voices blending together with mine on "Stand Up." I loved God's plan so much!

Near the end of the song, the singers were asked to add anything they "heard" improvisationally. Several individuals took a turn individually at the microphone. The Navy veteran said he "heard" a phrase that he believed needed to be spoken in the song. Since God gave him the phrase, he was asked to record it. In the final mix, Michael Everett placed the phrase at the beginning of the song.

When we had finished recording, Grace surprised me with a birthday cake, and all rallied around to celebrate my birthday with me. I was deeply touched! The greatest surprise of all, though, was learning that that particular Saturday (the third Saturday of May) was Armed Forces Day! Here I thought the Lord had prompted me to reserve the studio for May 19 as a birthday gift to me, but it was also to align the recording with the day which celebrated all those serving. Magnificent!

DAY 25

DATE: ____________________

SELECT

Before Daily Listening to Song Prayers

Select where on the album you want to begin listening,
set the album on shuffle, or move to a different album or playlist.

REFLECT

Before Daily Listening

Circle your current subjective emotional well-being.

One indicates lowest and ten highest.

1 2 3 4 5 6 7 8 9 10

What's going on for you today?

LISTEN

During-Listening Doodle and Coloring Space

REFLECT

After Daily Listening

Circle your current subjective emotional well-being.

One indicates lowest and ten highest.

1 2 3 4 5 6 7 8 9 10

What did you sense or notice?

What did you feel or experience?

What if any thoughts came to mind while listening?

What songs or lyrics stood out?

What is God speaking to you through today's listening? Do you have words for it?

... and they shall be His people and God shall personally be with them and be their God. (Rev. 21:3)

26

RESTORE

The seemingly crazy nudges from the Holy Spirit kept coming to continue developing more music. This felt crazy because the twenty-three songs already developed or in development between *Ascend in Worship*, *Walk on Water* and "Stand Up" remained almost completely unknown. I would not actually have *Walk on Water* CDs to hand out or ship until autumn 2007, yet already in December 2006, the inner nudge had come to begin work on additional songs for yet a third album. During the February recording session where we had initiated the rock anthem arrangement of "Stand Up" and the song for those grieving the fallen, "You Carry Me," as the final song for *Walk on Water*, we also initiated the first song prayers for *Restore.*

I did feel crazy. Who *does* this? Was the continued recording about my ego, or was I truly hearing from God as I thought? I did think it was God. I did, or I would not have kept going. Meanwhile, through expanding connections within the worship community, I was becoming aware of so many singers, musicians, and worship leaders who yearned to develop music in a professional studio, yet here I was doing it, and they were not. I could not understand that.

Now, working on my third album, I did not see myself as either a singer or recording artist, though according to common definition of the terms they could have been applied to me. (I still don't consider myself as these things.) I was just me, doing the best I could to obey what I thought was God's assignment. I felt completely dependent on His power for the work to have the effect He wanted it to and to reveal the wonder of His presence through whatever He knew I lacked.

God continued to expand within my heart a longing for more of us to meet with and live aware of the Holy Spirit, coming to rest and be restored in the flow of His river—flowing with Him through life as He flowed through us. This would be the renewal spoken of in Isaiah (Isa. 43:19). This would result in the restoration God had promised and that Jesus had initiated: Spirit-filled, Spirit-formed, Spirit-led lives! This third album would include song prayers calling on God to cause His Spirit to have an even greater effect on dry and thirsting hearts, so that His way of love would expand throughout the earth. This expansion would never be complete until eternity, but Jesus came so the restoration could begin now.

Eagles Nest Foundation was making progress toward being officially established. An attorney who was also a parent at our children's school volunteered to help me with non-profit paperwork.

Grace and I continued to work closely together supporting each other in our respective calls from God, always worshiping God musically as a foundational lifestyle before all else. One day, Grace spoke to me what she thought the Holy Spirit was saying. She did not think the song prayers God was having me create would be used for corporate worship but were for more personal use. I was devasted because beyond radio and corporate worship, that was the only use for song prayers that I could imagine.

On July 7, 2007, I was back in the studio working on the next songs for *Restore*. *Stand Up* was done. I was waiting on receipt of the completed CDs. Meanwhile, *Walk on Water* was in the final stages of completion.

DAY 26

DATE: ____________________

SELECT

Before Daily Listening to Song Prayers

Select where on the album you want to begin listening,
set the album on shuffle, or move to a different album or playlist.

REFLECT

Before Daily Listening

Circle your current subjective emotional well-being.

One indicates lowest and ten highest.

1 2 3 4 5 6 7 8 9 10

What's going on for you today?

LISTEN

During-Listening Doodle and Coloring Space

REFLECT

After Daily Listening

Circle your current subjective emotional well-being.

One indicates lowest and ten highest.

1 2 3 4 5 6 7 8 9 10

What did you sense or notice?

What did you feel or experience?

What if any thoughts came to mind while listening?

What songs or lyrics stood out?

What is God speaking to you through today's listening? Do you have words for it?

God will wipe away every tear from their eyes, and death shall be no more, neither shall there be anguish sorrow and mourning nor grief nor pain anymore ... (Rev. 21:4)

27

THRONE ROOM

My life continued, solely to the rhythm of worship, pray, listen, obey. As shared in the *Ascend in Worship Daily Listening Companion*, in the 1990s I reached a breaking point trying to juggle all of life's supposed "have-to's" according to seemingly logical deadlines. Fail, fail, fail! I was failing to meet the mark at work and managing our home with three children ages five and under. I knew God promised that He had a plan to prosper me and not to harm me. I knew God promised to share hidden knowledge with those who would seek Him. I knew that Jesus's sheep hear His voice. I surrendered my life to God's plan minute by minute. I only wanted His will, which means that I began listening all through the day to hear the inner promptings of the Holy Spirit. Then I would obey what I thought He was whispering. Of course, there was and is a learning curve to discern when you are hearing from God (and when you are not). I am still learning. In the meantime, though, I live by the four-word phrase He gave me that describes what followers of Jesus are called to do as a lifestyle: worship, pray, listen, obey.

You can worship God in many ways in your life, but I prefer to worship Him privately with song prayers each day. When I worship Him in song, the lyrics turn my thoughts toward God and gradually push out all lesser distractions. There in that place, with my thoughts oriented toward Him, I can more clearly hear His messages, and He touches my heart in ways I needed exactly at that given moment. Being in God's presence became like an addiction but one for which we were created. So, I embraced this place in and with Him as my true home and source of all I need to get through every day.

Two songs on *Walk on Water* speak to these core underlying beliefs: "We Enter His Throne Room" and "Your Throne is Mercy." Together, these two song prayers revel in our ability to come before God spiritually to adore Him and receive from Him. In His presence He feeds you what you need, nurtures your soul, and gives you His wisdom regarding what He wants next—as well as His strength to accomplish it.

"Your Throne is Mercy" adds to the spectacular privilege of being so welcomed and loved in His presence by recognizing the restoration cycle to which we are invited. As we come before Him in awe and bow to Him as King seeking forgiveness for all offenses, He sets us free. Then we join Him in prayer for the next people He wants to release from their spiritual and emotional prisons.

DAY 27

DATE: ____________________

SELECT

Before Daily Listening to Song Prayers

Select where on the album you want to begin listening,
set the album on shuffle, or move to a different album or playlist.

REFLECT

Before Daily Listening

Circle your current subjective emotional well-being.

One indicates lowest and ten highest.

1 2 3 4 5 6 7 8 9 10

What's going on for you today?

LISTEN

During-Listening Doodle and Coloring Space

REFLECT

After Daily Listening

Circle your current subjective emotional well-being.

One indicates lowest and ten highest.

1 2 3 4 5 6 7 8 9 10

What did you sense or notice?

What did you feel or experience?

What if any thoughts came to mind while listening?

What songs or lyrics stood out?

What is God speaking to you through today's listening?
Do you have words for it?

... He who is seated on the throne said, See! I make all things new ... (Rev. 21:5)

28

PATRIOTIC

I continued my daily obedience to worship, pray, listen, and then obey. Throughout each day, I constantly asked the Holy Spirit what He wanted me to do next. Where and how did He want me to spend my time? Doors began to open. I was sending emails and making phone calls, wherever He pointed out a possibility. As *Walk on Water* was in manufacturing, I received word of a Blue Star Mom pack-out to be held in Concord, California. I felt an inner nudge pushing me to attend. I obeyed.

As I stood in the assembly line packing boxes for deployed troops, I longed to say something about the resources God had had me create for the troops to provide spiritual support through listening to song prayers. However, I was unsure whether I should. The Blue Star Moms' information had been clear. Discussion about anything religious—at least the way I understood it—was not allowed.

Still, I felt the Spirit's nudge as I stood in between two of the members to mention the spiritual resources. After hesitating for a few minutes, I could not help but obey and awkwardly tried to share. The women were very interested in what I had to say and urged me to head across the room to let a particular Marine mom in the group know what I had just told them. I did as they suggested.

Judy was lovely and intrigued by what I shared. She invited me to meet at her office a short time later. She worked at a Presbyterian church in nearby Walnut Creek. I posited the possibility of presenting a day retreat for the women that I had developed for a California Moms in Prayer leadership called, *Exfoliating Worry*. She embraced the idea, and we set a date for August 18, 2007.

I set about re-designing the retreat booklet I had written the year prior specifically for the military moms. I felt the Holy Spirit's inner nudge to decorate the front cover with a heart that had a patriotic look and began searching the Internet. I found exactly the right one and went to the artist's website to inquire about usage. As only God could set up, through asking me to search for a patriotic heart, God had a gift for me. The artist, Kenneth Columella, was an Air Force veteran. He made all his patriotic art available to me for Eagles Nest Foundation, including the patriotic heart, and volunteered to design Eagles Nest's first logo.

The first order of CDs with the new rendition of "Stand Up" arrived within a few days of the retreat for the military moms at Judy's church. It would also be Judy who several months later connected me more deeply to the Gold Star family community.

Oh-so-slowly word was spreading that I prayed for military and their families. I received two urgent email prayer requests. One was for the son of the couple whose son had been deployed to Iraq when we recorded the troops singing for troops in May. There had been an IED explosion. They feared he had been killed. The truth was complex. Their son had not died. But the son of another family had.

The second email prayer request was for Sergeant Sam. Unrelated to the prior prayer request, his vehicle in Iraq had been hit. Others who were with him had died. He was not expected to live. His wife, Erin, was rushed to his side as they flew him from the battlefield to Germany. Would I keep praying? Yes, I would.

DAY 28

DATE: ____________________

SELECT

Before Daily Listening to Song Prayers

Select where on the album you want to begin listening, set the album on shuffle, or move to a different album or playlist.

REFLECT

Before Daily Listening

Circle your current subjective emotional well-being.

One indicates lowest and ten highest.

1 2 3 4 5 6 7 8 9 10

What's going on for you today?

LISTEN

During-Listening Doodle and Coloring Space

REFLECT

After Daily Listening

Circle your current subjective emotional well-being.

One indicates lowest and ten highest.

1 2 3 4 5 6 7 8 9 10

What did you sense or notice?

What did you feel or experience?

What if any thoughts came to mind while listening?

What songs or lyrics stood out?

What is God speaking to you through today's listening?
Do you have words for it?

Let us then fearlessly *and* confidently *and* boldly draw near to the throne of grace ... That we may receive mercy ... and ... [appropriate help and well-timed help, coming just when we need it.] (Heb.4:16)

29

RADIO

Now that the new arrangement of "Stand Up" was complete, the Holy Spirit nudged me to make the effort to get the patriotic song on the radio as many places as possible for the sixth memorial (on September 11, 2007) of the 9/11 terrorist attacks. A Northern California Christian radio station, KYCC, offered to support the effort by broadcasting the song on their network and pre-taping a radio interview with host, Theresa Schaad, for that day as well.

Since the "Salt and Light" weekend almost one year prior, Tamara and I had been in close touch again. Our main subject was always prayer. We prayed for one another. We prayed for our families. We prayed as the Holy Spirit led, and we prayed for our communities, the nations, and the world.

The Holy Spirit nudged me to call Tamara to see if she knew of anyone connected to a radio station who might be willing to broadcast "Stand Up" on September 11, 2007 as well. However, despite frequent contact, Tamara and I almost never telephoned. Other forms of electronic communication were less disruptive to our primary roles at the time as wives and mothers. I felt an insistent nudge from God, though, that I should call her. Reluctantly, I obeyed. Of course, Tamara was available to talk. (If you haven't noticed already, God knows what He is doing.) She did not know anyone in radio, but the fact that I had telephoned versus texting enabled the conversation to go easily in other directions. We talked about the military in general and then about Tamara's cousin, Cindy, whose son had had an accident and as a result had been in a coma. In what seemed an almost miraculous chain of events, he had recovered.

Immediately, Sam came to mind and his wife, Erin, who was at his bedside. I shared with Tamara the prayer request which had come and the current circumstances. She asked if I thought Erin might like to talk to someone whose loved one had recovered well from a coma. I answered that I thought she would. Tamara asked in which hospital Sam was at this time. I responded that he had been moved from Germany to Bethesda Naval Hospital in Maryland. Tamara paused, stunned. Her cousin could do more than a phone call. If she wanted, she would be able to visit Sam and Erin personally. Of all places, Cindy happened to live in Maryland in easy driving distance of the hospital.

At Tamara's urging, I telephoned Cindy to let her know about Sam. Cindy was excited to perhaps encourage Erin and looked forward to trying to drive to the hospital to visit. However, Cindy shared more. She and a group of friends were active every weekend with troop support activities. Would I be interested in coming the weekend around September 11, 2007, to Washington, DC to participate in the activities with them? There might be opportunity to find open doors for the song, "Stand Up." She invited me to stay with her husband and her at their home.

Meanwhile, at my house in California in our backyard, a new fiberglass pool was being filled with water. It was part of an overhaul to our backyard that would finally include a sprinkler system for the struggling lawn as well. Water! Water was being brought into a wasteland at exactly the time I has having these phone calls. It seemed God was continuing to let me know that I was in His will and to keep going. (Worship, pray, listen, obey …)

DAY 29

DATE: ____________________

SELECT

Before Daily Listening to Song Prayers

Select where on the album you want to begin listening,
set the album on shuffle, or move to a different album or playlist.

REFLECT

Before Daily Listening

Circle your current subjective emotional well-being.

One indicates lowest and ten highest.

1 2 3 4 5 6 7 8 9 10

What's going on for you today?

LISTEN

During-Listening Doodle and Coloring Space

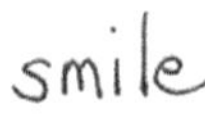

REFLECT

After Daily Listening

Circle your current subjective emotional well-being.

One indicates lowest and ten highest.

1 2 3 4 5 6 7 8 9 10

What did you sense or notice?

What did you feel or experience?

What if any thoughts came to mind while listening?

What songs or lyrics stood out?

What is God speaking to you through today's listening?
Do you have words for it?

For as the heavens are higher than the earth, so are My ways higher than your ways and My thoughts than your thoughts. (Isa. 55:9)

30

TAKE-OFF

The first week of September 2007, Eagles Nest Foundation was officially incorporated by the State of California. On September 8, I was to leave for about a week in Washington, DC, staying with Tamara's cousin, Cindy, and participating in activities to commemorate the attacks on September 11, 2001. We would remember those who valiantly served and those who lost their lives that day.

This trip had come together once again in a way that was astounding. For instance, God had nudged me to call Tamara to try to get "Stand Up" on the radio instead of texting or emailing her. This call about our troops and what God's plans might be for them had led to Tamara sharing about the injury and subsequent amazing healing journey of her cousin Cindy's son. God had then nudged me that perhaps Cindy's story about her son could encourage Erin, Sam's wife, while he still lay in a coma.

Next had come the realization that Cindy lived close enough to the hospital where Sam lay, to personally visit. Then came the conversation with Cindy inviting me to come to Washington, DC and stay with her in order to see what connections might be made the week of September 11, 2007 to get the word out regarding the song, "Stand Up."

A day or so after I affirmed I would make the trip to Washington, DC, a card arrived from my grandmother stating that she wanted to share a bit of money with each of her grandchildren. It was exactly the amount I needed for the plane ticket across the country!

I felt beyond excited as I boarded the plane. In my suitcase were multiple copies of "Stand Up" and *Ascend in Worship* to hand out to whomever God pointed out to me. I had wanted to email or call the chaplain at the Pentagon who had taken my call in mid-2005 regarding my efforts to try to get songs to the troops. He had politely informed me that if I ever got the songs on CD to reconnect with him. Well, here I was with CDs in hand, and I was headed to Washington! I ran out of time, though, to let him know.

My local California newspaper had interviewed me for an article about releasing "Stand Up," which would appear on September 11, 2007, while I was gone to DC. The radio interview regarding the song by KYCC's disc jockey, Theresa, was scheduled to air on September 11 as well. Airing of the interview would immediately be followed by broadcast of the rock anthem arrangement of "Stand Up."

As I sat on the first flight waiting for it to taxi down the runway, the Holy Spirit dropped the thought into my mind that this trip was like a countdown to some type of launch. I was thrilled.

DAY 30

DATE: ____________________

SELECT

Before Daily Listening to Song Prayers

Select where on the album you want to begin listening,
set the album on shuffle, or move to a different album or playlist.

REFLECT

Before Daily Listening

Circle your current subjective emotional well-being.

One indicates lowest and ten highest.

1 2 3 4 5 6 7 8 9 10

What's going on for you today?

LISTEN

During-Listening Doodle and Coloring Space

REFLECT

After Daily Listening

Circle your current subjective emotional well-being.

One indicates lowest and ten highest.

1 2 3 4 5 6 7 8 9 10

What did you sense or notice?

What did you feel or experience?

What if any thoughts came to mind while listening?

What songs or lyrics stood out?

What is God speaking to you through today's listening?
Do you have words for it?

... those who wait for the Lord [who ... hope in Him] shall change *and* renew their strength *and* power; they shall lift their wings *and* mount up [close to God] as eagles ... (Isa. 40:30a)

APPENDIX

RESOURCES

ADDITIONAL COMPANION JOURNALS

- *Ascend in Worship*
- *Best Life*
- *Courage*
- *Legacy*
- *Restore*
- *Walk on Water*

FURTHER RESOURCES BY DR. ELIZABETH

Books

- *Learning to Love (Not Loathe) Me*
- *Only Jesus Remains: Reflections for Tending Hurting Hearts at Christmas*
- *Truth: Spiritual Manual for Battle*
- *Soul Care-Song Prayers: A Spiritual Practice Toward Resilience and Well-Being*
- *Santa Claus Celebrates Jesus's Birthday*
- *The Tree—a little book of faith and hope (coming in 2026)*
- *Bunny at the Cross (coming in 2026)*
- *Don't Stay at the Manger (coming in 2026)*
- *New Year's Light (coming for 2027)*

Song Prayer Albums

- *Ascend in Worship*
- *Walk on Water*
- *Restore*
- *God Seeker*
- *Resurrection Joy*
- *You're My Healer*
- *My Dwelling Place*
- *Eternity*
- *Even Now*
- *Beginning and the End*
- *King of My Heart*
- *Fly Like an Eagle*
- *Courage*

- *God in Darkness*
- *Best Life*
- *Legacy*
- *Road's Not Easy*
- *Hymns One*
- *Hymns Two*
- *No Words (instrumental)*
- *No Words Two (instrumental)*
- *On Earth as in Heaven*
- *Adore*

Christmas Song Prayer Albums

- *Christmas Worship*
- *Christmas Bells Call to Worship*
- *Child of Wonder*
- *So You Sent Your Son*
- *In the Fullness of Time*
- *How Hard was the Night*
- *Once Upon a Time*

Podcasts

- *God Seeker Messages*
- *Military Faith and Spiritual Resilience*

Substack

- Subscribe: https://substack.com/@drelizabethfulgaro
- Monthly newsletter
- Blog
- Sneak Peeks
- Live Streaming Events

Visit www.elizabethfulgaro.com to find updates and learn more.

BLANK JOURNALING PAGES

ABOUT THE AUTHOR

Dr. Elizabeth Fulgaro cares deeply about people and their well-being. She develops materials for soul care with an emphasis on inner healing. Dr. Elizabeth is an award-winning author and has recorded over 250 original song prayers on 25+ albums. Her song prayers open up a liminal space where listeners can meet with God to receive what they need from Him. She is driven to understand God more and communicate what she learns to others. Fulgaro is Founder and CEO of Eagles Nest Foundation, Inc. (501c3) which provides spiritual support through her albums and playlists of song prayers, books, devotions, and podcasts.

Dr. Elizabeth has a mission to serve military, military families, veterans, and anyone going through other types of battles. She earned her Doctor of Ministry degree from The King's University (2023) and Spiritual Direction certification (2025). She also holds a Master of Practical Theology (2019) and a Bachelor of Arts (1979) in German Language and Literature from California State University, Sacramento.

Dr. Elizabeth has been married to John since 1981. They live in the Sierra Nevada foothills of Northern California, where they enjoy going on long walks. They have three adult children. When she is not writing and recording, Dr. Elizabeth relaxes with playing piano, needlepoint, learning foreign languages, and time in the company of her husband, adult children, and friends, who are like family all over the world.

Made in the USA
Coppell, TX
30 December 2025